Words for Students of English

Vocabulary Series Editors
Holly Deemer Rogerson
Lionel Menasche

Volume 7

WORDS
for Students of English

A Vocabulary Series for ESL

Holly Deemer Rogerson

**University of Pittsburgh Press for the English Language Institute
of the University of Pittsburgh**

First published by the University of Michigan Press 1993
Copyright © 1990, University of Pittsburgh Press and
   the English Language Institute, University of Pittsburgh
All rights reserved
ISBN 0-472-08217-5
Published in the United States of America by
The University of Michigan Press
Manufactured in the United States of America

2000   1999   1998   1997   6   5   4   3

Contents

Foreword

The objective of this series of vocabulary texts for the student of English as a foreign language is to facilitate the learning of approximately 3,000 new base words. Vocabulary learning has long been deemphasized in language teaching, much to the detriment of the students, who have mostly been left to fend for themselves. We thoroughly agree with Muriel Saville-Troike, who states, "Vocabulary knowledge in English is the most important aspect of oral English proficiency for academic achievement" (*TESOL Quarterly*, vol. 18, no. 2, p. 216).

With the present lack of comprehensive vocabulary texts suitable for both classroom use and home study, this series is intended to support teachers in preparing effective vocabulary lessons so that they can meet their students' urgent need for an increased lexicon. We present here a selection of base vocabulary items and some of their derived forms (i.e., the noun, verb, adverb, and adjective of the same stem) together with a series of exercises designed to help students remember the new words and use them in context.

This text has been used in an experimental edition in the English Language Institute, and modifications suggested by its use have been incorporated in the present version.

Christina Bratt Paulston
Director, English Language Institute
University of Pittsburgh

Acknowledgments

A series such as this depends greatly on the cooperation and hard work of numerous people:

Christina Bratt Paulston and Holly Deemer Rogerson originated the idea for the series.

Christina Bratt Paulston provided ongoing support for the series.

Mary Newton Bruder, Carol Jasnow, Christina Bratt Paulston, and Holly Deemer Rogerson developed the first version of the list of approximately 600 words assumed known.

Holly Deemer Rogerson developed the original pool of words from which the 150 topic word lists were chosen. She also organized the word lists and, with Lionel Menasche, provided general management of the project, including authors' drafts, revisions, editing, illustrations, duplicating, testing, and typing.

Ideas for word lists, format, and exercise types were contributed by Betsy Davis, Gary Esarey, Suzanne T. Hershelman, Carol Jasnow, Carol Moltz, Lionel Menasche, Holly Deemer Rogerson, Dorolyn A. Smith, and Linda M. Schmandt.

Lionel Menasche and Holly Deemer Rogerson were responsible for final revisions of content with input from classroom testing by Isabel Dillener, Jeanette Courson, Caroline Haessly, Pat Furey, Carol Jasnow, Ken Rose, Linda M. Schmandt, Jill Sherman, Joe Sukenik, Tom Swinscoe, and Lois Wilson.

Marilyn S. Butler reviewed a preliminary version of Volume 7 and made many useful suggestions for improvements in exercises.

Courtenay Meade Snellings and Dexter Kimball provided valuable editorial assistance in content revision and proofreading.

JoEllen Walker and Anna Mae Townsend typed several drafts of the manuscript.

Lisa Krizmanich assisted during the testing phase.

Introduction

Volume 7 of *Words for Students of English* continues the graded presentation of English vocabulary beyond the 3,000 basic words introduced in the first six volumes of the series. This volume introduces about 300 new words for production and 400 for recognition. In each of the twenty-two units, there are approximately fourteen new words for production and eighteen for recognition.

Many features of the initial six volumes have been retained: Each unit centers on a topic so that students have an appropriate context for each new word. Carefully graded exercises follow the definitions and example sentences in each unit, providing ample opportunity to practice the new vocabulary. Answer keys are provided for approximately half of the exercises to allow for individual study and practice.

Format

Each unit has the following sections:

WORDS FOR PRODUCTION	WORDS FOR RECOGNITION
Word Form Chart	Key Words and Synonyms
Definitions and Examples	Examples
Exercises	Exercises

For each unit, there is also a review exercise, either within the unit itself or in combination with a later unit on the same topic.

Words for Production and Recognition

The advanced nature of the vocabulary covered in Volume 7 and the special needs of advanced learners have led to the division of the words into two groups: words to be learned primarily for use in speaking and writing—the production skills—and those presented primarily for listening and reading—the recognition skills. While it is not possible to establish a clear psycholinguistic division between words for production and for recognition, there are pedagogical advantages in doing so for advanced ESL students.

At the advanced level, students have an increased need to acquire a very broad recognition vocabulary. For most general concepts, advanced students already know at least one word which they can use when speaking or writing, but they need to recognize a much larger corpus of words referring to similar concepts if they are to understand normal spoken and written English. For example, advanced students who have learned to understand and use the word *secretly* need to understand the similar concepts represented by *furtively* and *surreptitiously*. It is the premise of this book that the students' time is better spent in learning to associate *furtively* and *surreptitiously* with *secretly*, a relatively easy task, than in attempting to learn the exact distinctions in meaning and use between these three words, a very difficult task for most students.

Thus, words referring to concepts for which students are unlikely to know synonymous words (for example, *embezzle*) are presented for production, with full definitions and example sentences, followed by exercises leading to productive use of the word in the students' speech and writing. However, words like *convict* and *inmate*, for which students undoubtedly know the simpler word *prisoner*, are presented only for recognition, and the focus of the presentation and exercises is strictly on helping the students to remember the association of *convict* and *inmate* with *prisoner*. Once a student "knows" the word *inmate*, in the sense of recognizing its basic meaning as similar to that of *prisoner*, he or she may come across it frequently and also learn to use it in appropriate contexts. However, this text leaves that phase of learning to each student, and concentrates on presenting a large number of words for recognition in order to facilitate students' listening and reading in English, activities through which they can continue to expand their vocabularies even after their formal English study ends.

Suggestions for Teachers

The division of each unit into production words and recognition words allows for flexibility of use. According to the needs and level of the class, a teacher may wish to cover only the production words. A teacher whose class includes students of varying proficiencies may wish to require only the higher level students to study the recognition words. It is also possible to have the students cover only the production words during one term, and then study the recognition words during an ensuing term, thereby providing an automatic delayed review of the production words. Whatever approach is used, teachers should be aware that the recognition exercises may seem somewhat easy to the students. They are cognitively less complex than the production exercises because the task of associating new words with known key words is itself a relatively simple task.

When given words to learn only for recognition, some students, unaccustomed to the idea, may want to know the subtle distinctions between the words. In this case the teacher must decide whether the students' questions stem from lack of familiarity with the new approach or whether they are proficient enough in English to absorb and retain the answers to such questions. In the former case, the teacher should reiterate the value of initially studying very advanced vocabulary solely for recognition: a large recognition vocabulary makes reading and listening more efficient and opens the door to further progress in English for advanced students. In the latter case, the teacher may wish to explain those synonyms which he or she feels do have significant differences in their meaning, or the students may be assigned to look them up in a good monolingual English dictionary and then create and discuss sentences which show the differences in meaning or usage.

Words for Students of English

Crime (A)

WORDS FOR PRODUCTION

Word Form Chart

NOUN	VERB	ADJECTIVE	ADVERB
alibi			
assassination	assassinate	assassinated	
assassin			
assault	assault	assaulted	
counterfeit	counterfeit	counterfeit	
counterfeiter			
embezzlement	embezzle	embezzled	
embezzler			
felony		felonious	feloniously
felon			
interrogation	interrogate	interrogated	
interrogator			
	lurk	lurking	
misdemeanor			
perjury	perjure		
perjurer			
revenge	revenge		
revenger			
torture	torture	tortured	
torturer			

Definitions and Examples

1. **alibi** [the fact or state of having been somewhere else at the time of a crime; a reasonable excuse intended to avoid blame or punishment]

    His alibi is that he was in the hospital on the day the murder took place.

2. **assassinate** [to murder, especially to murder a government official or public person]

    President John F. Kennedy was assassinated in 1963.
    The assassin used a high-powered rifle to shoot him.
    The assassination occurred during a parade in Texas.
    The assassinated president was mourned by people all over the world.

3. **assault** [to attack] (*assault* is the word used by U.S. courts of law for *attack*.)

    He assaulted and killed an old man during the robbery.
    She was charged with assault after she hit the other woman.

4. **counterfeit** [to make an imitation of something with the intent to deceive]

    That money is counterfeit; it is worthless.
    The counterfeit money was burned by the police.
    The counterfeiters had a printing press in the basement where they had made the fake stamps.
    Those supposedly "designer" clothes are counterfeits; they were not made by a famous designer.

5. **embezzle** [to take money entrusted to your care and use it illegally]

    Over a period of five years, he embezzled more than a million dollars from the bank where he worked.
    His embezzlement was not discovered until he ran away to Brazil.
    The embezzled money was never recovered.
    Unfortunately, the club's treasurer was an embezzler, and the club no longer has any money.

6. **felony** [a serious crime for which there is a strict punishment]

    Murder and armed robbery are felonies.
    That felon was convicted of robbery.
    His intent was not felonious when he took the money, but he was convicted of embezzlement and sent to jail.

7. **interrogate** [to question formally and systematically]

    The police are trained in methods of effective interrogation.
    They shone a bright light in his eyes when they interrogated him.
    The two interrogators alternated asking me questions.
    The interrogated people were later released.

8. **lurk** [to wait in a place of concealment, especially for an evil purpose]

   The robbers lurked in the bushes outside of the house until the owners left.
   The lurking man was spotted by the police.

9. **misdemeanor** [a crime that is not as serious as a felony]

   He only had to pay a fine because possession of such a small amount of illegal drugs was a misdemeanor.

10. **perjury** [lying in a court of law, where one has sworn to tell the whole truth]

    He committed perjury when he stated that he had had no knowledge of his friends' criminal intent.
    Be careful not to perjure yourself with your testimony.
    A perjurer's testimony is of no value to the court.

11. **revenge** [to cause injury in return for injury]

    The man wanted revenge against his wife's attacker and tried to kill him.
    She promised her father before his death that she would revenge his death.
    He wanted to be the revenger of all his family's troubles.

12. **torture** [to (purposely) cause pain]

    The kidnappers tortured and killed their victim when they realized that the ransom money was counterfeit.
    The police are not supposed to use torture when they are interrogating a prisoner.
    The robbery victim was tortured by memories of what had happened.

Exercises

A. Write **T** if the sentence is true and **F** if it is false.

_____ **1.** The police suspect the people with no alibis.

_____ **2.** Embezzlement is a white-collar crime.

_____ **3.** Counterfeit money has no real value.

_____ **4.** The police may suspect people who lurk near dark alleys.

_____ **5.** A felony is more serious than a misdemeanor.

_____ **6.** You should believe a perjuror.

_____ **7.** An assassin kills people.

_____ **8.** An assault is a misdemeanor.

_____ **9.** Torture is painful.

B.   Answer each question with a word from the word form chart on page 3.

  1. What methods might be used to get information from prisoners?
  2. What is murder an example of?
  3. Who kills important people?
  4. Who steals money from his or her own company?
  5. What kind of crime is not serious?
  6. What will cause a person to feel pain?
  7. What may the victim of a crime want?
  8. Who lies in a court of law?
  9. What do you need if you are accused of a crime?
 10. What does an attacker do to his victim?
 11. What kind of money is fake?

C.   Circle the word that is least related in meaning.

  1. perjure   assassinate   murder
  2. fake   felon   counterfeit
  3. embezzle   wait   lurk
  4. misdemeanor   alibi   excuse
  5. steal   assassinate   embezzle
  6. lie   perjure   assault
  7. lurk   hurt   torture
  8. question   interrogate   embezzle
  9. assault   attack   counterfeit

D.   In the blanks, write the most appropriate words from the word form chart on page 3.

  1. The attacker _____ in the shadows in the park until his victim walked by.
  2. The _____ currency looked quite real, but a careful inspection showed it to be worthless.
  3. She committed _____ with her false testimony.
  4. The parents of the murdered boy wanted his killer executed because they wanted _____ for his death.
  5. The police think that the missing money was _____ ; they think that the bank manager took it.
  6. She does not have to go to prison because the crime was only a(n)

     _____ .

  7. President Kennedy was killed by a(n) _____ .

   8. The prisoner refused to answer the questions of the _____ .

   9. His _____ is that he was in school when the crime was committed.

10. The thief _____ outside of the apartment building until he was sure that the building was empty.

E.   Answer the following questions.

   1. Name two crimes which are only misdemeanors in your country.

   2. Have any political figures in your country been assassinated? Explain.

   3. Do you think that a crime committed in revenge by the victim of a crime is ever justified? Explain.

   4. Give an example of an effective alibi.

   5. How can a person avoid being assaulted?

   6. How does the government try to prevent the production of counterfeit money? How successful are these methods?

   7. How can you tell when a person is lurking, and not simply waiting?

   8. Why do employees sometimes embezzle from their own companies? Do you think that embezzlement is as serious a crime as robbing a bank? Why or why not?

WORDS FOR RECOGNITION

KEY WORD	SYNONYMS
attacker (n)	assailant
lurk (v)	skulk
prison (n)	jail, penitentiary, reformatory, stockade
prisoner (n)	convict, inmate
revenge (n)	vengeance, retribution
scream (v)	holler (colloq.), shout, yell
secretly (adv)	furtively, surreptitiously

Example Sentences

attacker

The woman said that she could not describe her assailant because it had been dark when the attack had taken place.

lurk

The police found two members of the gang skulking around the warehouse.

prison

The police bring the prisoner from the jail to the courthouse each morning.
She is serving a five-year sentence in a federal penitentiary.
The teenage boys were sent to a reformatory for youthful offenders.
The accused soldiers were taken to the military stockade to await their trial.

prisoner

The convicts are confined to their cells except at mealtimes.
The inmates are demanding better food and more exercise time.

revenge

He hated John Carter so much that he took vengeance against the entire Carter family by burning their house down.
In retribution for being fired, she stole some money from the cash register in the store where she had worked.

scream

The kidnap victims hollered continuously until someone heard and came to release them.
The rioters shouted at the police who tried to control them.
The interrogators yelled at the prisoner to try to scare him.
The woman shrieked when she saw the man lurking in the shadows.

secretly

> The assassin furtively took out his gun and aimed at his target.
> The embezzler surreptitiously changed the amounts in the records to conceal his theft.

Exercises

F.   Circle the word that is least related in meaning.

1. yell   holler   pummel   shout
2. penitentiary   menace   stockade   reformatory
3. furtive   weird   surreptitious
4. attacker   inmate   assailant
5. holler   convict   inmate   prisoner
6. lurk   skulk   yell

G.   Write the key word for each set of words.

1. furtively   surreptitiously   _____
2. convict   inmate   _____
3. penitentiary   stockade   _____
4. jail   reformatory   _____
5. holler   shout   _____
6. retribution   vengeance   _____
7. shout   yell   _____

H.   Write the key word which corresponds to each italicized word.

1. The kidnapped man *hollered* for help. _____
2. His victims want *retribution* against him. _____
3. He was seen *skulking* around the victim's home. _____
4. Her *assailant* was a teenage boy. _____
5. His *furtive* actions caused suspicion. _____
6. The *inmates* are complaining about the food. _____
7. The police heard a sudden *shriek*. _____
8. That *reformatory* is far from the city. _____
9. The murder was an act of *vengeance*. _____
10. One of the *convicts* escaped. _____

I. Choose all the possible antonyms for each word from the group of words below and write them on the line.

1. defender _____

2. public _____

3. whisper _____

skulk	jail	yell
holler	furtive	shout
stockade	assailant	surreptitious
vengeance	penitentiary	inmate

J. Write **T** if the sentence is true and **F** if it is false.

_____ **1.** People sometimes yell because they are angry.

_____ **2.** Convicts in prisons often carry guns.

_____ **3.** Skulking around is an example of suspicious behavior.

_____ **4.** An assaulted person may want retribution.

_____ **5.** If his victim yells, an assailant may flee.

_____ **6.** A penitentiary has inmates.

_____ **7.** Hollering is a furtive action.

_____ **8.** A man will be sent to a stockade for a misdemeanor.

_____ **9.** A successful embezzler must be surreptitious.

_____ **10.** A tortured person may want vengeance.

K. Answer the following questions.

1. Do you think that it is a good idea to holler if you are being assaulted? Why or why not?

2. Describe how inmates in penitentiaries in your country are treated.

3. What would you do if you saw a man lurking around your neighborhood?

4. Are youthful offenders in your country sent to reformatories?

5. What can you do to protect yourself against assailants?

6. What would you do if you were sitting in your home at night and heard a shriek outside?

7. Describe some behavior that you consider to be furtive.

8. Are any convicts allowed out of prisons in your country? Under what circumstances?

9. Which crimes require surreptitious behavior on the part of the criminal?

Review Exercise

L. Choose the appropriate words from the charts on pages 3 and 8 to answer the following questions.

1. Which two nouns refer to broad categories of crimes?

   _____   _____

2. Which two nouns refer to people?

   _____   _____

3. Which five verbs refer to a type of speech?

   _____   _____   _____

   _____   _____

4. Which four nouns refer to places?

   _____   _____

   _____   _____

5. Which two verbs refer to crimes that are definitely related to money?

   _____   _____

Work (A)

WORDS FOR PRODUCTION

Word Form Chart

NOUN	VERB	ADJECTIVE	ADVERB
		adamant	adamantly
adversity		adverse	adversely
aimlessness		aimless	aimlessly
	botch	botched	
	dawdle	dawdling	
errand			
grimness		grim	grimly
		grueling	gruelingly
impediment	impede		
ineptness		inept	ineptly
	mollify	mollified	
shift			
tardiness		tardy	tardily
underling			

Definitions and Examples

1. **adamant** [unyielding; immovable, especially in opposition]

   The boss was adamant in his refusal to approve the plan.
   She adamantly demanded a raise.

2. **adverse** [unfavorable; opposed to one's interests]

> I admire her ability to succeed in the face of adversity.
> The adverse market conditions will affect the sales of our product.
> Your behavior will adversely affect the boss's opinion of you.

3. **aimless** [without definite purpose]

> The workers dislike the aimlessness of these contract negotiations; they want a specific agenda of topics to be agreed on.
> Her research efforts so far have been rather aimless; she needs to examine her goals more carefully and then proceed.
> After the closing of the factory had been announced, the workers walked around the plant aimlessly and discussed the sad news with their friends.

4. **botch** [to do in a hopelessly bad way]

> He was fired because he botched each of his assignments.
> We tried to figure out how to repair the botched job he had done.

5. **dawdle** [to waste time]

> She had dawdled all morning and did not complete her task by noon.
> The dawdling workers quickly settled down to work when their supervisor entered the plant.

6. **errand** [a short trip to take care of some business]

> I spend most of my day running errands for the boss so that she does not have to leave the office.

7. **grim** [unhappy; with little hope]

> The grimness of their situation was obvious at the sales meeting.
> The union leaders looked grim as they called the meeting to order.
> They grimly demanded to see the boss.

8. **grueling** [difficult to the point of exhaustion]

> The workers are saying that the new, faster pace of the assembly line is grueling.
> He worked gruelingly long hours in order to complete the project on schedule.

9. **impede** [to interfere with the operation of]

> The worst impediment to my advancement at work is my boss's negative attitude toward me.
> Our progress is being impeded by difficulties in obtaining the necessary raw materials.

10. **inept** [incompetent; generally lacking in aptitude or suitability]

    Her ineptness brings her constant criticism.
    He was initially inept but gradually learned to do his job well.
    He ineptly attempted to assemble the machine but was unable to.

11. **mollify** [to calm or soothe; to make less severe]

    Their mollification did not last for long; soon they were griping again
      about the poor working conditions in the factory.
    The strikers were not mollified by the meager pay increase offered by the
      company.

12. **shift** [a scheduled period of work or duty; a change of one group of workers for
    another in regular alternation]

    He is working the day shift this week and finishes at 3:30 P.M.

13. **tardy** [late]

    He has been reprimanded for his chronic tardiness.
    My supervisor notices if I am tardy.
    He does his work, but always tardily.

14. **underling** [one who is under the orders of another; a subordinate]

    She is in charge of a large group of underlings in her new position.

Exercises

A. Write **T** if the sentence is true and **F** if it is false.

    _____ **1.** An inept worker may botch his job.

    _____ **2.** Adverse circumstances will not impede a project.

    _____ **3.** Most errands are dangerous.

    _____ **4.** Supervisors do not like workers to work aimlessly.

    _____ **5.** Laughing at a person mollifies that person.

    _____ **6.** Supervisors encourage their workers to dawdle.

    _____ **7.** A typical factory has about ten shifts per day.

    _____ **8.** Dawdling makes people tardy.

    _____ **9.** It is difficult to win an argument against someone who is
            adamant.

    _____ **10.** Supervisors should be able to enumerate the job responsibilities of
            those they supervise.

    _____ **11.** People look grim when they are pleased with something.

    _____ **12.** A person needs to be strong to complete a grueling job.

    _____ **13.** Underlings usually give orders.

B.   Answer each question with a word from the word form chart on page 12.

    1. What are you if you arrive late?
    2. How can you describe a job that has not been skillfully done?
    3. Who may run errands for a superior?
    4. What kind of circumstances make a job difficult?
    5. How may you speak if you feel strongly about your topic?
    6. What may cause you to be tardy?
    7. What kind of worker may botch a job?
    8. What kind of task may exhaust workers?
    9. How do people look immediately after a disaster?
   10. What is something that prevents you from accomplishing a goal?
   11. How do people walk if they do not know where to go?
   12. What is 9:00 A.M. to 5:00 P.M. an example of?

C.   Circle the word that is least related in meaning.

    1. ruin   dawdle   botch
    2. inept   clumsy   aimless
    3. tardy   grim   worried
    4. adverse   negative   mollified
    5. mollify   botch   calm
    6. servant   underling   supervisor
    7. impede   interfere   mock
    8. difficult   adamant   grueling
    9. aimlessness   enumeration   list
   10. shift   errand   hours

D.   Complete each analogy with a word from the word form chart on page 12.

    1. theft : felony :: _____ : work
    2. skillful : succeed :: inept : _____
    3. general : private :: boss : _____
    4. difficult : exam :: _____ : task
    5. strong : push :: _____ : words
    6. nonsense : speech :: _____ : work

E. In the blanks, write the most appropriate words from the word form chart on page 12.

1. His face looked _____ as he examined the damage in the factory.

2. She has no ideas of her own; she is only one of the boss's

_____ .

3. He works so _____ that he never actually accomplishes anything.

4. The lack of fuel is _____ our production in the plant.

5. The union leaders had a meeting with the company officials last night and _____ the complaints of the workers.

6. His ineptness caused him to _____ the job.

7. My work _____ starts at midnight and finishes at 8:00 A.M.

8. The boss will not tolerate his _____ any longer; the next time he is late, he will be fired.

9. She was not _____ by her co-worker's apology and was still angry when she went home.

F. Answer the following questions.

1. When do you tend to dawdle?
2. Describe some task at which you are inept.
3. Describe some of the impediments that you may face in your career plans.
4. Have you ever really botched something? Describe the situation.
5. If your boss is angry with you, what do you think is a good way to mollify him or her?
6. Name something that you are adamant about. Why do you feel this way?
7. What jobs do you think are particularly grueling? Why?
8. What shift would you prefer to work? Why?
9. What do you think are the advantages of being an underling?

WORDS FOR RECOGNITION

KEY WORD	SYNONYMS
agree (v)	acquiesce, assent
aimless (adj)	desultory
adverse (adj)	calamitous, dire, inimical, ruinous, untoward
botch (v)	bungle
dawdle (v)	dally, dillydally, linger
diligent (adj)	assiduous, punctilious, unflagging
grim (adj)	dour, solemn, somber
impede (v)	hamper, hinder
mollify (v)	appease, assuage, temper
underling (n)	minion

Example Sentences

adverse

> The fire in the factory resulted in a calamitous situation.
> The dire prediction of the owner came true when the factory closed.
> His plan is inimical to our purposes.
> The effects of the fire were ruinous to their plans.
> Various untoward circumstances forced the closing of the store.

agree

> In the face of such strong opposition, the management decided to acquiesce and offer a new contract.
> The union leaders assented to the government's demand that the workers return to their jobs.

aimless

> Her desultory manner makes me think that she is not interested in her job.

botch

> The boss was angry when I bungled my assignment.

dawdle

> The boss caught her dallying instead of working.
> If we dillydally any more, we will not finish on time.
> He lingered over his coffee and got back to work late.

diligent

> She assiduously attended to all the tasks related to the work.
> His attitude toward his tasks is always punctilious.
> Her unflagging attention to her duties makes her an excellent worker.

grim

> His dour expression warned me that he was annoyed at my question.
> The atmosphere in the shop has been solemn ever since our adverse situation became clear.
> The funeral workers wore somber black uniforms.

impede

> Our production is hampered by equipment that does not function properly.
> My supervisor's poor opinion of my work will certainly hinder my progress in the company.

mollify

> The union will not be appeased by this offer.
> Her wrath was assuaged by his promise to repair the damage.
> His suggestion of overtime pay tempered their negative attitude toward their heavy schedule.

underling

> My boss always has his minions do all of the work for him, instead of doing it himself.

Exercises

G.   Circle the word that is least related in meaning.

1. desultory   inimical   dire   untoward
2. solemn   assent   dour   somber
3. unflagging   assiduous   ruinous   punctilious
4. temper   appease   assuage   bungle
5. dally   bungle   linger   dawdle
6. appease   acquiesce   assent   agree

H. Write the key word for each set of words.

1. hamper   hinder   _____
2. ruinous   calamitous   _____
3. linger   dally   _____
4. assiduous   unflagging   _____
5. dire   untoward   _____
6. temper   assuage   _____
7. solemn   somber   _____

I. Write the key word that corresponds to each italicized word.

1. They *assented* to our demands. _____
2. His anger was momentarily *tempered.* _____
3. These conditions are *inimical* to our project. _____
4. She *lingered* over her meal. _____
5. He is always so *dour.* _____
6. She sent one of her *minions* to do it. _____
7. They are always *dillydallying* around. _____
8. The boss will be angry if you *bungle* this. _____
9. Her efforts were *desultory*, and she accomplished little.

_____

J. Choose all the possible antonyms for each word from the group of words below and write them on the line. The antonyms should be the same part of speech as the cue word.

1. hurry _____
2. happy _____
3. anger (v) _____
4. help _____
5. lazy _____
6. purposeful _____

acquiesce	assuage	dillydally
somber	assiduous	linger
temper	appease	hinder
hamper	unflagging	dally
solemn	dour	punctilious
assent	desultory	

K. Write **T** if the sentence is true and **F** if it is false.

_____ 1. An abrasive personality will hamper a person's ability to get along well with others.

_____ 2. Assiduous workers often bungle their jobs.

_____ 3. A somber attitude may be caused by dire circumstances.

_____ 4. A person's anger may be assuaged by a sincere apology.

_____ 5. If your work is done in a desultory manner, you will quickly be promoted.

_____ 6. People acquiesce when they can no longer resist.

_____ 7. Untoward circumstances hamper the progress of a project.

_____ 8. Minions are normally in charge of important projects.

L. Answer the following questions.

1. When are you likely to dillydally? Why?
2. When are you most punctilious? Why?
3. When do you usually feel solemn? Why?
4. How do you try to appease an angry friend?
5. Describe a time when your efforts were desultory.
6. Have you ever been someone's minion? Explain.
7. What has hindered your progress in English?

War (A)

WORDS FOR PRODUCTION

Word Form Chart

NOUN	VERB	ADJECTIVE	ADVERB
ambush	ambush	ambushed	
barracks			
camouflage	camouflage	camouflaged	
casualty			
civilian		civilian	
deserter	desert	deserting	
desertion			
garrison			
hostility		hostile	hostilely
loot	loot	looted	
looter			
mercenary			
raid	raid	raiding	
raider		raided	
retaliation	retaliate	retaliatory	
sabotage	sabotage	sabotaged	
saboteur			
siege	besiege	besieged	
truce			

Definitions and Examples

1. **ambush** [a trap in which concealed people lie in wait to attack by surprise]

    During the ambush at the bend in the road, armed men jumped out of bushes by the road and forced the truck to stop.
    They ambushed the small group as it entered the woods.
    Almost half of the ambushed soldiers were killed or wounded.

2. **barracks** {usually plural} [a building or set of buildings used to house soldiers]

    There were 100 beds in the barracks.

3. **camouflage** [concealment by means of disguise, especially that of military equipment by paint, nets, or vegetation]

    The camouflage of the trucks was very effective; we could not see them until we were only a few meters away.
    We must camouflage our tents so that they cannot be seen from the air.
    The camouflaged troops were not visible to the enemy.

4. **casualty** [a person lost through death, wounds, sickness, or capture]

    There were several hundred casualties in that battle; we need some replacement troops.

5. **civilian** [a person not in the military]

    Unfortunately, not only soldiers, but also civilians, are often hurt and killed during wars.

6. **desert** [to abandon military service without permission]

    The deserter ran away from the battle.
    The military police are looking for him because he deserted.
    The deserting men burned their uniforms and stole some civilian clothing.
    Desertion from the military during a war is sometimes punished by death.

7. **garrison** [a military post or installation, especially a permanent one]

    The civilians felt safe because there was a large garrison at the edge of their town.

8. **hostility** [of or relating to an enemy; very unfriendly]

    There is a lot of hostility toward the occupation army; several of the troops have been killed when they went out of their barracks alone.
    The invaders will punish any hostile act.

9. **loot** [goods of value taken by force]

> Jewels and valuable paintings were included in the loot taken from the house by the soldiers.
> The men looted the kitchen and stole all of the remaining food.
> The looted silver will never be recovered.

10. **mercenary** [a person who serves only for wages in a foreign military]

> Their army is filled with mercenaries because their own civilians do not want to serve in the military.

11. **raid** [a surprise attack by a small force]

> The raid on the garrison by the rebels was successful; they captured all of the weapons and ammunition held there.
> They decided to raid the stockade during the night in order to free the prisoners.
> The raiding party wore black paint on their faces as camouflage.
> One of the raided ships sank in the harbor.
> The raiders killed several civilians.

12. **retaliate** [to repay an injury in a similar manner; to take revenge]

> The attack was retaliation for the explosion which had killed twenty people.
> The government wants to retaliate quickly against the guerrillas.
> The occurrence of one retaliatory act after another by both sides has pushed the country closer and closer to civil war.

13. **sabotage** [a destructive action designed to hinder a nation's war effort]

> The explosion of the bridge was an act of sabotage by the guerrillas.
> If they sabotage the country's communication system, panic will result.
> The sabotaged airport was in ruins.
> The saboteurs put explosives under the railroad tracks.

14. **siege** [a military isolation of a city or area in order to force it to surrender]

> The siege of the town lasted for two weeks but ended when the food supply ran out and the town garrison surrendered.
> They plan to besiege the city for as long as it takes to force the residents to give up.
> The people in the besieged area were dying because they had no more medical supplies.

15. **truce** [a suspension of fighting by agreement between opposing forces]

> The signing of the truce ended the five-year war between the two countries.

Exercises

A.   Write **T** if the sentence is true and **F** if it is false.

_____ **1.** A garrison may contain several barracks.

_____ **2.** Saboteurs often must camouflage themselves.

_____ **3.** A truce is usually the beginning of a war.

_____ **4.** A mercenary fights primarily because of his political beliefs.

_____ **5.** Soldiers give loot to the people they have conquered.

_____ **6.** A high casualty rate is good.

_____ **7.** The military punishes soldiers who try to desert.

_____ **8.** An ambush is a type of surprise.

_____ **9.** Officers in the military are civilians.

_____ **10.** People are hostile toward their enemies.

B.   Answer each question with a word from the word form chart on page 21.

1. What may soldiers take from civilians?
2. What may people want to do after being attacked?
3. Who leaves the army without permission?
4. What may cause a city to surrender?
5. What may end a war?
6. What is a person killed in a battle an example of?
7. Where do soldiers live? (two answers)
8. Who may fight for a country other than his own?
9. Who is not in the military?
10. What type of attack requires the attackers to hide and wait for their victims?

C.   Circle the word that is least related in meaning.

1. soldier   mercenary   civilian

2. ambush   retaliation   revenge

3. camouflage   hide   raid

4. besiege   sabotage   damage

5. hostility   dormitory   barracks

6. death   casualty   loot

7. attack   garrison   raid

8. contract   truce   ambush

D.   Complete each analogy with a word from the word form chart on page 21.

1. wreck : car :: _____ : soldier

2. drop out : school :: _____ : army

    3. dormitory : students :: _____ : soldiers

    4. mask : face :: _____ : truck

    5. white : black :: _____ : soldier

E. In the blanks, write the appropriate word from the word form chart on page 21.

    1. The invading army _____ the city for five days, but the citizens refused to surrender.

    2. He _____ from the army because he did not want to kill anyone.

    3. The explosion at the radio station was an act of _____ .

    4. A _____ containing 500 men protects the town.

    5. They put leaves on the top of the barracks in order to _____ them.

    6. The commander told his men that he would not permit any _____ in the captured town; anyone caught with stolen goods would be severely punished.

    7. The two-week _____ ended when the fighting resumed last night.

    8. _____ were high during that battle: over 1,000 killed and 3,000 wounded.

    9. Our government has threatened to _____ quickly if the enemy attacks.

    10. The _____ between the two groups was evident; they could not even talk without immediately beginning to argue.

    11. The small group of saboteurs planned a night _____ on the ammunition warehouse.

    12. As the troops entered the supposedly empty town, they were _____ by the guerrillas who were hiding there.

F. Answer the following questions.

    1. What is the penalty for desertion from the military in your country?
    2. Do civilians in your country have any rights that members of the military do not have? Explain.
    3. Do any foreign mercenaries serve in your country's military? Explain.
    4. Should governments retaliate against terrorists? How?
    5. What kinds of camouflage do soldiers in your country use? Why?
    6. Has your city ever experienced a siege? Explain.
    7. Should soldiers be permitted to loot? If not, how can looting be prevented?
    8. Which war in the history of your country resulted in the most casualties?
    9. What conditions do you think are necessary for an effective truce?

WORDS FOR RECOGNITION

KEY WORD	SYNONYMS
enemy (n)	adversary, foe
guard (n)	sentry
hostility (n)	animosity, enmity, rancor
loot (n)	booty, plunder, spoils
loot (v)	pillage, plunder
raid (n)	foray, incursion
retaliation (n)	reprisal
surrender (v)	capitulate, cede, hand over, relinquish
trick (n)	ruse, subterfuge
truce (n)	armistice, cease-fire

Example Sentences

enemy

That country is our strongest adversary.
Their foes are determined to defeat them.

guard

Two sentries were standing at the gate.

hostility

They bear us much animosity because of the last war.
The enmity between those two countries threatens to break out into war at any moment.
They overcame their once deep rancor and became friends.

loot

The invaders took much booty from the town.
They piled their plunder in the truck and drove away.
The soldiers searched the area for spoils.

loot

They pillaged the captured city.
The soldiers plundered wherever they went.

raid

Only twenty men went on the foray deep into enemy territory.
Their incursion into the town last night resulted in heavy casualties on both sides.

retaliation

In swift reprisal against the raid, the rebel quarters were bombed.

surrender

After weeks of fighting, the rebel army capitulated.
As part of the truce, the southern portion of the city was ceded to the rebels.
They were forced to hand their weapons over to their captors.
They fought bravely, but eventually relinquished their hold on the city to the
  rebels.

trick

Their supposed retreat was only a ruse to trap the soldiers following them.
Their subterfuge was successful: the soldiers walked right into their ambush.

truce

Each year we celebrate the day of the armistice that marked the end of the war.
A cease-fire was called during the five-day holiday.

Exercises

G.   Circle the word that is least related in meaning.

    1. ruse   armistice   cease-fire

    2. rancor   booty   animosity

    3. pillage   hand over   relinquish

    4. adversary   foe   spoils

    5. plunder   sentry   pillage

    6. subterfuge   foe   ruse

    7. adversary   animosity   enmity

    8. incursion   foray   armistice

H.   Write the key word for each set of words.

    1. booty   plunder   _____

    2. enmity   rancor   _____

    3. armistice   cease-fire   _____

    4. adversary   foe   _____

    5. incursion   foray   _____

    6. subterfuge   ruse   _____

    7. pillage   plunder   _____

    8. cede   relinquish   _____

I.   Write the key word which corresponds to each italicized word.

  1. The *sentry* stood by the gate. _____

  2. The attack was in *reprisal* for the civilians' deaths. _____

  3. The *foray* across the border lasted for three hours. _____

  4. Everyone hopes that the *cease-fire* will last. _____

  5. The village was *plundered.* _____

  6. Their *ruse* was successful, and we were surprised. _____

  7. The rebels refused to *capitulate.* _____

  8. We fear our *adversaries.* _____

  9. The *booty* was worth a lot of money. _____

  10. He earned our *enmity* with his actions. _____

  11. They *relinquished* the town after two weeks of fighting. _____

  12. Our *foes* are dangerous. _____

J.   Write **T** if the sentence is true and **F** if it is false.

  _____ **1.** Soldiers never want plunder.

  _____ **2.** The side which is winning will usually capitulate.

  _____ **3.** A foray lasts a long time.

  _____ **4.** People often have to fight against their foes.

  _____ **5.** An armistice often causes many deaths.

  _____ **6.** A ruse is supposed to fool people.

  _____ **7.** Loot is often valuable.

  _____ **8.** A reprisal is usually the first in a series of hostile acts.

  _____ **9.** An incursion requires a very large number of soldiers.

  _____ **10.** A sentry's job is to watch an area in order to protect it.

K.   Answer the following questions.

  1. What characteristics do you think a good sentry should have?
  2. What circumstances are necessary for an effective cease-fire?
  3. Has your country ever been forced to relinquish part of its territory? Explain.
  4. What types of items do you think are attractive to invading soldiers as booty? Explain.
  5. Give a factual example of a reprisal. Was it effective?
  6. Do you have any particular adversaries at school or in sports? Explain.
  7. Under what circumstances do you think it is wise for an army to capitulate?
  8. Give a historical example of a successful ruse.

Family (A)

WORDS FOR PRODUCTION

Word Form Chart

NOUN	VERB	ADJECTIVE
adolescent		adolescent
adolescence		
adoption	adopt	adopted
conflict	conflict	conflicting
custody		
descendant	descend	
descent		
embrace	embrace	
		foster
guardian		
	nurture	nurturing
scolding	scold	
spanking	spank	
temperament		temperamental
toddler	toddle	
ward		

Definitions and Examples

1. **adolescent** [a person between the approximate ages of twelve and twenty]

    Many adolescents wish that they were already adults.
    His adolescent behavior bothered the adults.
    Some people look back fondly on their adolescence and wish that they
      could be teenagers again.

2. **adopt** [to take by choice into one's family]

   They were unable to have children and adopted a six-month-old baby.
   Their two boys have light hair, but their adopted daughter has dark hair.

3. **conflict** [a hostile encounter]

   Their two-year marriage was full of conflict; they were always arguing.
   My father's ideas on politics conflict with mine; we never agree.
   They have conflicting views on how to raise children.

4. **custody** [direct charge and control exercised by a person or an authority]

   When the boy's parents died, his grandparents were given custody of him.

5. **descendant** [one who comes from another]

   He says that he is a descendant of an eighteenth-century English king.
   Many of the wild horses in America are descended from the horses that
     the Spanish explorers brought with them in the sixteenth century.
   She is of German descent; her great-grandparents came to this country
     from Germany 100 years ago.

6. **embrace** [to hold (a person) close in one's arms]

   He held his wife in a tight embrace as he said good-bye.
   She embraced her granddaughter and kissed her on the cheek.

7. **foster** [receiving parental care although not related by blood or legal ties]

   That family has had a foster child for the past six months; they plan to
     keep her until a suitable family is found to adopt her.

8. **guardian** [one who is in charge of a person or some property]

   The family lawyer became the children's guardian when the rest of the
     family was killed in a car accident.

9. **nurture** [to provide with those things necessary for growth, such as food or
   education]

   Children need to be nurtured in a variety of ways if they are to become
     well-adjusted adults.
   A nurturing environment is one in which the child is able to learn, grow,
     and feel positive about himself.

10. **scold** [to strongly and verbally criticize another's (usually a child's) behavior]

    The mother gave the little girl a scolding when she saw the paint on the
      floor.
    He scolded the boy for hitting his sister and sent him to his room.

11. **spank** [to hit, especially on the seat, with an open hand]

    He gave the little boy a spanking for disobeying his mother.
    Some parents never spank their children, but others frequently do.

12. **temperament** [a characteristic or habitual tendency of emotional response]

    She has a very even temperament; she rarely gets angry.

13. **temperamental** [showing quickly changing and unpredictable moods]

    The temperamental child refused to say hello to the visitors.

14. **toddler** [a young child who is learning or has recently learned to walk]

    The mother held her toddler by the hand as they slowly crossed the street.
    The baby is just beginning to toddle around; soon he will be able to walk
    more steadily.

15. **ward** [a person under the guard or care of another]

    Those children are wards of the state now because all of their family are
    dead.

Exercises

A. Write **T** if the sentence is true and **F** if it is false.

_____ 1. Most people like to be embraced by their loved ones.

_____ 2. A guardian takes care of a ward.

_____ 3. Children enjoy being scolded.

_____ 4. Parents normally have custody of their children.

_____ 5. A person's parents are his descendants.

_____ 6. A toddler is older than an adolescent.

_____ 7. When people adopt a child, they then have custody of that child.

_____ 8. You must spank children frequently in order to nurture them.

_____ 9. A person's temperament determines his general mood.

B. Answer each question with a word from the word form chart on page 29.

1. Name two things that a parent might do to a disobedient child.
2. Who is slightly older than an infant?
3. Who will your grandchildren be?
4. Who is in charge of a ward?
5. Who is close to being an adult?
6. What is an argument an example of?
7. What may family members do to each other when they meet?
8. What should parents try to do to their children?
9. What is a way to get a child?
10. Concerning their children, what may divorcing parents argue about?
11. What kind of child is neither legally adopted nor blood-related to its
    parents?

C. Circle the word that is least related in meaning.

    1. descendant   child   toddler

    2. guardian   ward   parent

    3. teenager   adolescent   embrace

    4. conflict   problem   temperament

    5. scold   educate   nurture

    6. custody   spanking   responsibility

    7. grandson   grandfather   descendant

    8. spank   scold   hit

D. Complete each analogy with a word from the word form chart on page 29.

    1. grandfather : ancestor :: grandson : _____

    2. infant : toddler :: _____ : adult

    3. hands : handshake :: arms : _____

    4. father : son :: _____ : ward

    5. touch : hit :: speak : _____

    6. scold : voice :: _____ : hand

E. In the blanks, write the most appropriate words from the word form chart on page 29.

    1. My grandmother is very _____ ; one minute she is happy, and the next she is upset about some small problem.

    2. The divorcing parents both want the child, so the court will have to decide who will get _____ .

    3. That mother is very busy because she has both an infant and a(n) _____ to take care of.

    4. Psychologists say that married couples can reduce the _____ in their relationships by communicating more openly with each other.

    5. _____ children are legally part of the family but are not related by blood to the rest of the family.

    6. When my brother was a(n) _____ , he had a lot of arguments with our father.

    7. My older brother was my legal _____ after my parents died.

    8. My sister tries to avoid all _____ ; she hates to argue.

9. My parents did not believe in using physical punishment; while they often _____ me, they never _____ me.

10. People have many different ideas about the best way to _____ children, but everyone agrees that parents must show their children that they love them.

F. Answer the following questions.

1. Do people in your country commonly adopt children? Under what circumstances?
2. What do you think are the major sources of conflict within families in your country?
3. Do you think that spanking is an appropriate punishment for a toddler? Explain.
4. Do the members of your family embrace often? Explain.
5. After a divorce in your country, which parent usually gets custody of the children? Explain.
6. What do you think is the best way to nurture a child?
7. How would you describe your temperament?

WORDS FOR RECOGNITION

KEY WORD	SYNONYMS
conflict (n)	discord, dissension, friction, strife
cry (v)	sob, wail, whimper
descent (n)	stock, lineage
embrace (v)	cuddle, hug
raise (v)	rear
scold (v)	admonish, chastise, reprimand
temperament (n)	disposition

Example Sentences

conflict

They are experiencing a lot of discord over their decision not to take a vacation.
A period of dissension followed the initial argument.
There is often friction between a woman and her mother-in-law.
This strife is bound to end in open fighting.

cry

The woman sobbed as she watched her child's burial.
The child began to wail when she saw her balloon drift away.
He whimpered in fear as the bear approached.

descent

Many people of French stock live in the southern part of the United States.
Some people like to trace their lineage as far back as they can find records.

embrace

The father cuddled the little boy until he stopped crying.
My mother and father always hug before he leaves for work in the morning.

raise

Many psychologists say that it is best for children to be reared in a home where both parents are present.

scold

   He admonished the children when they begged the visitor for presents.
   The child was chastised for his behavior and sent to sit in the corner.
   The teacher reprimanded the students for talking during the test.

temperament

   She has a very sunny disposition; she is always smiling, even during difficult
      times.

Exercises

G.   Circle the word that is least related in meaning.

   1. admonish   sob   chastise

   2. hug   cuddle   reprimand

   3. strife   discord   stock

   4. wail   whimper   admonish

   5. chastise   reprimand   cuddle

   6. stock   lineage   rear

   7. dissension   disposition   friction

   8. wail   raise   rear

H.   Write the key word for each set of words.

   1. reprimand   chastise   _____

   2. cuddle   hug   _____

   3. discord   strife   _____

   4. sob   whimper   _____

   5. friction   dissension   _____

   6. lineage   stock   _____

   7. whimper   wail   _____

   8. chastise   admonish   _____

I.   Write the key word which corresponds to each italicized word.

   1. The woman *cuddled* the child in her arms. _____

   2. They *reared* their children quite strictly. _____

   3. He has a pleasant *disposition*. _____

   4. The *dissension* within that family is evident. _____

5. He sharply *adominished* the noisy children. _____

6. She is researching the *lineage* of the family. _____

7. The *whimpering* child held my hand. _____

8. She hates being *chastised*. _____

9. There is constant *strife* between those two groups. _____

10. She *sobbed* as she read the letter. _____

11. He *hugged* his mother and then left. _____

12. He is of Irish *stock*. _____

J. Write **T** if the sentence is true and **F** if it is false.

_____ 1. Children enjoy being cuddled by their parents.

_____ 2. Friction helps a family.

_____ 3. To rear your children correctly, you should constantly chastise them.

_____ 4. People may sob when they are unhappy.

_____ 5. Children enjoy being reprimanded by their parents.

_____ 6. People are often happy or sad according to their dispositions.

_____ 7. The Chinese and the French share a common lineage.

_____ 8. A child who is whimpering needs to be cuddled.

K. Answer the following questions.

1. Describe your best friend's disposition.
2. Are people in your country interested in their lineage? Explain.
3. Were you reared strictly? Explain.
4. Do you think that it is a good idea to reprimand children in public? Explain.
5. What do you think are the most common sources of friction in workplaces?
6. Which members of your family do you frequently hug? Under what circumstances?
7. When you were a child, what did your parents frequently admonish you about?

Housing (A)

WORDS FOR PRODUCTION

Word Form Chart

NOUN	VERB	ADJECTIVE
annex	annex	annexed
awning		
disposal	dispose of	disposable
ghetto		
	lean	leaning
mansion		
palace		palatial
pantry		
partition	partition	
pillar		
ramp		
renovation	renovate	renovated
shed		
tenement		
ventilation	ventilate	ventilated

Definitions and Examples

1. **annex** [a supplementary structure, often attached to a building]

    The county courthouse is no longer large enough, so they have started to use the courthouse annex, which is one block away.

    (b) [to take or obtain for oneself]

    The United States annexed parts of northern Mexico during the nineteenth century.
    The annexed land is still part of the United States.

2. **awning** [a rooflike cover, often made of canvas, which extends over an area or a window as a shelter]

    The windows on the front of the house have awnings that are used to keep out the summer sun.

3. **dispose of** [to get rid of]

    Many large cities have difficulty finding adequate, safe ways to dispose of their garbage.
    Paper cups are disposable; you throw them away after you use them once.
    Many American homes have garbage disposals in the kitchen sinks that automatically dispose of all food waste.

4. **ghetto** [a part of a city in which mainly minority group members live, often because of social, legal, or economic pressure]

    Many people who live in ghettos dream of moving out.
    Low incomes and poor housing are typical ghetto problems.

5. **lean** [to slant from a vertical position]

    The telephone pole had fallen over and was leaning against the house.
    The Leaning Tower of Pisa is a famous tourist attraction in Italy.

6. **mansion** [a large, impressive house]

    That wealthy family lives in a mansion in the nicest section of town.

7. **palace** [the official house of a ruler]

    The area around the palace is well guarded to protect the royal family.
    He has a lot of money and is planning to build a house which will be palatial.

8. **pantry** [a room or closet used for storing food or plates, glasses, etc.]

    She went into the pantry to get the bread for dinner.

9. **partition** [something that divides, especially an interior dividing wall]

    The partition separated the dining room from the living room.
    We are planning to partition this very large room to make two rooms.

10. pillar [a firm, upright support for a structure]

Four pillars supported the roof of the porch.

11. ramp [a sloping floor, walk, or roadway leading from one level to another]

There was a ramp next to the stairs for wheelchairs to use.

12. renovate [to restore to a former, better state]

The renovations on the old house are almost complete; it looks like new.
We will need to totally renovate the barn; it is falling down now.
Renovated homes in this area of the city are bringing good prices.

13. shed [a small structure built for storage or shelter]

My father keeps the yard tools in a shed in the backyard.

14. tenement [an apartment house with poor standards of sanitation, safety, and comfort, and occupied by poor families in a city]

He grew up in a tenement in a ghetto of a large city.

15. ventilation [the circulation of air]

Good ventilation is required for a safe kitchen.
That fan in the wall ventilates this room.
The best ventilated rooms in this apartment are the bedrooms.

Exercises

A. Write **T** if the sentence is true and **F** if it is false.

_____ 1. Many people want to live in mansions.
_____ 2. New buildings need renovation.
_____ 3. Clothes are kept in pantries.
_____ 4. Pillars support a building.
_____ 5. Buildings should lean a lot.
_____ 6. Most people live in ghettos.
_____ 7. People dispose of things that they do not want.
_____ 8. A king often lives in a palace.
_____ 9. An awning can protect a window from the sun.
_____ 10. A tenement is a nice apartment.
_____ 11. An annex may be an addition to a building.
_____ 12. A ramp can take the place of a stairway.

B. Answer each question with a word from the word form chart on page 37.

    1. What divides a space?
    2. Where may people keep tools?
    3. What do windows provide?
    4. Where do many people not like to live? (two answers)
    5. What kind of house is very nice? (two answers)
    6. What room is often next to the kitchen?
    7. What may cover a porch?
    8. What may a poorly constructed building do?
    9. What may support the roof of a building?

C. Circle the word that is least related in meaning.

    1. partition   apartment   tenement
    2. cover   ramp   awning
    3. pantry   storeroom   palace
    4. remove   renovate   restore
    5. shed   mansion   house
    6. annex   awning   addition
    7. district   ghetto   disposal

D. Complete each analogy with a word from the word form chart on page 37.

    1. garbage : food :: _____ : neighborhood
    2. scissors : cut :: window : _____
    3. tools : shed :: dishes : _____
    4. roof : house :: _____ : porch

E. In the blanks, write the appropriate word from the word form chart on page 37.

   1. The old queen almost never leaves her _____ .

   2. There is not enough air in this room; it needs more _____ .

   3. The girls wheeled their bicycles up the _____ in front of the building.

   4. The older part of the building dates to 1900, but the _____ is a much more recent addition.

   5. Be careful to _____ these chemicals properly. Do not simply pour them down the drain.

   6. That area of the city has become a _____ for recent immigrants.

   7. The _____ shaded the porch.

   8. That old _____ is worth more than a million dollars, but no one is living in it now.

   9. My mother always told me not to _____ on the dinner table with my elbows.

   10. A _____ separated the two parts of the room.

   11. The garden hose is in the _____ .

F. Answer the following questions.

   1. What are the sources of ventilation in your apartment/house?
   2. Are there any ghettos in this city/town? Explain.
   3. Where are there mansions in this city/town?
   4. How do people here dispose of their trash? Their garbage?
   5. Is it acceptable manners in your country to lean on the table while you are eating?
   6. Does this city/town have ramps to help handicapped people get around? Where?
   7. Does the ruler of your country live in a palace? Describe it.
   8. Name a famous building in your country that has pillars. Describe it.

WORDS FOR RECOGNITION

KEY WORD	SYNONYMS
attic (n)	garret, loft
build (v)	erect
building (n)	edifice
dirt (n)	grime, filth
home (n)	domicile, dwelling, residence
lean (v)	list, tilt
pantry (n)	larder
porch (n)	patio, veranda
shelter (n)	refuge

Example Sentences

attic

He lives in a garret apartment.
We store the extra furniture in the loft.

build

They are planning to erect several buildings on this land.

building

That office building is the largest edifice in town.

dirt

The old kitchen was covered with grime.
The filth in the cellar will have to be cleaned out.

home

His domicile is in the capital city.
That house is a two-family dwelling.
They have a summer residence at the beach.

lean

The foundation of that house is weak, and it is starting to list to the right.
The pillars on that porch are tilted; they need to be straightened.

pantry

There is more sugar in the larder.

porch

> There is a patio at the back of that house.
> They are having the party out on the veranda.

shelter

> She took refuge from the storm in an abandoned house.

Exercises

G. Circle the word that is least related in meaning.

1. residence   dwelling   larder
2. patio   loft   veranda
3. domicile   filth   grime
4. edifice   garret   loft
5. tilt   erect   list
6. domicile   residence   refuge
7. pantry   edifice   building
8. shelter   refuge   dwelling

H. Write the key word for each set of words.

1. grime   filth   _____
2. loft   garret   _____
3. domicile   dwelling   _____
4. tilt   list   _____
5. veranda   patio   _____
6. residence   domicile   _____

I. Write the key word which corresponds to each italicized word.

1. I have no permanent *domicile*. _____
2. *Grime* from the car covered his face. _____
3. Under a tree is not a good place of *refuge* during a storm.

    _____

4. The ship was *listing* after the accident. _____
5. The *veranda* is surrounded by flowers. _____
6. That is an imposing *edifice*. _____
7. A statue was *erected* in her honor. _____
8. The *garret* is *filthy*. _____ _____
9. Put the eggs in the *larder*. _____
10. My old clothes are in the *loft*. _____

J. Write **T** if the sentence is true and **F** if it is false.

_____ 1. A veranda is inside a house.

_____ 2. Food may be kept in larders.

_____ 3. Your domicile is where you live.

_____ 4. A patio is outside of a house.

_____ 5. People want grime in their houses.

_____ 6. An edifice is at the top of a house.

_____ 7. Pillars that support houses should tilt.

_____ 8. An apartment house is a multiple-family dwelling.

_____ 9. Filth is a form of refuge.

K. Answer the following questions.

1. What is a good place of refuge during a thunderstorm?
2. What is the largest edifice in the capital of your country?
3. Do houses in your country typically have larders?
4. What are patios useful for?
5. Do houses in your country usually have garrets?
6. Where is your permanent residence?

Review Exercise

L. Read the passage and fill in the blanks with the appropriate words from the chart on page 37. Then answer the questions that follow.

The city's Urban Renewal Council announced today that it has purchased an old (1) _____ on Roosevelt Avenue. The house, erected in 1910 and now in poor condition, will be (2) _____ at the city's expense. It is located in the middle of one of the city's worst ghettos, where most of the inhabitants live in (3) _____ apartments which are in bad condition. The house, along with about thirty others like it on nearby streets, has been empty for more than ten years.

The URC's plans for the house are to put up (4) _____ in many of its larger rooms in order to create small apartments. The large garret of the house will also be converted into several apartments. Officials estimate that eventually the mansion will provide domiciles for nine families.

The first step in the renovation process will be to (5) _____ the filth that has collected in the house during the past ten years. Officials estimate that the completion of the renovations, including the installation of additional windows so that each dwelling will be properly (6) _____ , will take no more than six months.

1. How old is the house? _____

_____

2. What kind of housing surrounds the mansion? _____

_____

3. How will nine separate apartments be created in the house? _____

_____

4. Why are more windows to be put in? _____

_____

Education and Thought (A)

WORDS FOR PRODUCTION

Word Form Chart

NOUN	VERB	ADJECTIVE	ADVERB
apprentice apprenticeship	apprentice	apprenticed	
		apt	aptly
aptitude			
discernment	discern	discerning	discerningly
doctrine			
drawback			
inference	infer		
insight			
mumble	mumble	mumbled mumbling	
retardation	retard	retarded	
truancy			
truant		truant	
unruliness		unruly	

Definitions and Examples

1. **apprentice** [one who is learning by practical experience under skilled workers]

    She is working as an apprentice to a plumber; after she is trained, she hopes to join the plumbers' union.

    The apprenticed workers are not permitted to do any important jobs by themselves.

2. **apt** (a) [unusually fit or qualified]

   His comments on our situation were very apt; he obviously understands our problem clearly.

   (b) [having a tendency]

   Students are more apt to miss class in the spring when the weather is nice.

3. **aptitude** [capacity for learning]

   He is majoring in Russian because he has a high aptitude for languages.

4. **discern** [to detect with one's senses; to recognize mentally]

   The discernment of their target was difficult in the dark.
   She soon discerned the real reason for his request although he did not state it.
   It was very discerning of them to understand our problem before we explained it.

5. **doctrine** [a principle or position in a branch of knowledge]

   Many of the protesters follow Ghandi's doctrine of nonviolent resistance.

6. **drawback** [an objectionable feature; a hindrance]

   The major drawback to that plan is that it will require a large sum of money.

7. **infer** [to understand as a conclusion by reasoning from facts, rather than from direct statement]

   A variety of inferences are possible from the data which we currently have.
   She saw the smoke and inferred that there must be a fire.

8. **insight** [the power or act of seeing into a situation; discernment]

   Her insights on the dilemma have proven to be quite valuable.

9. **mumble** [to speak in a low, indistinct manner]

   His answer to the policeman's question was only a mumble.
   You should try not to mumble when you speak.
   I could not understand her mumbled answer.
   The mumbling elderly man was taken to the hospital.

10. **retard** [to slow up, especially by preventing or hindering]

    The many problems which we encountered retarded our progress on the project.

11. **retarded** [mentally handicapped]

    That is a special school for retarded children.

12. **truant** [one who stays out of school without permission]

> His teachers complain that he is a constant truant.
> The truant students spent the day at a shopping center.
> The school officials wish to lower the rate of truancy.

13. **unruly** [not easily disciplined or managed]

> The substitute teacher was upset by the unruliness of the class.
> She sent the most unruly students to speak to the principal.

Exercises

A. Write **T** if the sentence is true and **F** if it is false.

_____ 1. A good speaker mumbles.

_____ 2. People are good at things that they have a high aptitude for.

_____ 3. Teachers like unruly behavior.

_____ 4. An apprentice is learning a skill.

_____ 5. Being truant helps a student get good grades.

_____ 6. If a plan has many drawbacks, it is probably not a good plan.

_____ 7. A person who discerns the truth of situations has insight.

_____ 8. People who believe in a particular religion will try to follow its doctrines.

_____ 9. Students who study a lot are apt to get poor grades.

B. Answer each question with a word from the word form chart on page 46.

1. Who stays home from school too often?
2. What can you make based on facts?
3. Who works and learns at the same time?
4. What kind of behavior do parents object to?
5. What kind of speech is difficult to understand?
6. What does a psychologist need concerning patients' problems? (two answers)
7. What will being absent a lot do to a student's progress in school?

C. Circle the word that is least related in meaning.

1. ability   aptitude   apprentice
2. retard   mumble   speak
3. conclusion   drawback   inference
4. insight   discernment   truancy

    5. doctrine   drawback   problem

    6. apt   truant   absent

    7. retarded   apprenticed   slow

    8. undisciplined   unruly   unable

D. In the blanks, write the most appropriate words from the word form chart on page 46.

1. The _____ of that church specifies that members may not divorce.

2. Often students in junior high school take _____ tests which help show in which areas each student has potential.

3. The child _____ so badly that I could not understand a word he said.

4. In his job as the _____ officer for that school district, he must investigate the reasons for students' extended absences.

5. She is working as a(n) _____ in a newspaper office in order to learn how to run the printing presses.

6. The rain we have had recently has _____ the progress of the construction on that road.

7. Students who are often truant from school are _____ to quit school as soon as they reach the legal age to do so.

8. That article shows real _____ into the levels of meaning of that poetry.

9. The _____ to that system is that many jobs would be eliminated.

10. The _____ children were pushing each other and screaming as they waited in line.

E. Answer the following questions.

1. Where do you feel that your aptitude lies?
2. What are you apt to do when you have a free day?
3. What do you think has retarded your progress in English?
4. Which jobs in your country require a period of apprenticeship?
5. How should teachers deal with unruly classes?
6. What are the drawbacks to living in the capital city of your country?
7. Describe the central doctrines in your religion.

WORDS FOR RECOGNITION

KEY WORD	SYNONYMS
awareness (n)	cognizance
beginner (n)	novice
clear (adj)	lucid
confuse (v)	baffle, bewilder, perplex
doctrine (n)	dogma, tenet
fool (n)	dolt, idiot, imbecile, oaf
idea (n)	notion
mumble (v)	mutter
think (about) (v)	muse, ponder
wise (adj)	judicious, prudent

Example Sentences

awareness

Her cognizance of the root of her problem has not yet led to its solution.

beginner

He has only been playing golf for a few weeks, so he is still a novice.

clear

Her argument was quite lucid, and we all understood it.

confuse

He was baffled by many of the test questions and is sure that he failed.
I was bewildered by the size of the new school and had no idea how to find
    my classes.
The doctors have found this new disease to be perplexing; they are unsure of
    how to treat it.

doctrine

He is not thinking this through independently; he is only repeating the dogma
    that he has read.
One of the basic tenets of many religions is the need for people to treat others
    as they themselves prefer to be treated.

fool

> She was a dolt to lose all of her money gambling.
> He is an idiot not to wear his seatbelt when driving so fast.
> They think that she is an imbecile because she has spent years working on that project with no results.
> The other students think that he is an oaf because he is always dropping his books and papers on the floor and asking silly questions.

idea

> She has a notion about how to proceed on the project.

mumble

> No one understood him because he was muttering.

think

> She is musing over that problem now.
> We will have to ponder a bit before we come to a decision.

wise

> It would be judicious to study this problem carefully and not make any quick decisions.
> Prudent students begin their studying well before the exam.

Exercises

F.   Circle the word that is least related in meaning.

1. mutter   murder   mumble
2. novice   notion   thought
3. prudent   lucid   judicious
4. ponder   retard   muse
5. notion   idiot   oaf
6. mutter   perplex   baffle
7. dolt   tenet   imbecile
8. tenet   dogma   novice
9. perplex   bewilder   ponder
10. cognizance   awareness   dogma

G. Write the key word for each set of words.

1. imbecile   idiot   _____
2. ponder   muse   _____
3. dogma   tenet   _____
4. perplex   baffle   _____
5. dolt   oaf   _____
6. prudent   judicious   _____

H. Write the key word which corresponds to each italicized word.

1. His *lucid* description of the problem was admired by everyone.

   _____

2. The *notion* that attending class is not important is erroneous.

   _____

3. If you *mutter*, no one will hear you. _____
4. Her performance was excellent, for a *novice*. _____
5. He was told to *ponder* his future. _____
6. She recited the organization's basic *tenets*. _____
7. He was *bewildered* by the choices he faced. _____
8. It would be *judicious* to pay closer attention. _____
9. That *oaf* spilled his drink all over me. _____
10. She has shown no *cognizance* of the seriousness of this situation.

    _____

I. Choose all of the possible antonyms for each word from the group of words below and write them on the line. The antonyms should be the same part of speech as the cue word.

1. clarify _____
2. expert _____
3. stupid _____
4. confused _____

bewilder	novice	lucid	perplex
dogma	prudent	mutter	baffle
notion	muse	judicious	oaf

J. Write **T** if the sentence is true and **F** if it is false.

——— 1. A muttered explanation is easy to understand.

——— 2. A lucid explanation is easy to understand.

——— 3. An imbecile is usually prudent in his actions.

——— 4. The holy book of a religion often lists its tenets.

——— 5. People can hear another person pondering.

——— 6. A novice is usually very skilled.

——— 7. People may be baffled by strange notions.

——— 8. An idiot's decisions are not usually judicious.

K. Answer the following questions.

1. Are you cognizant of your own weaknesses as a student? Explain.
2. What area of English grammar perplexes you the most?
3. What are you a novice at? Do you intend to continue learning?
4. What do you do when you have something important to ponder?
5. What issue in the news right now do you find baffling?
6. What action would be judicious for your government to take at this time?
7. What is your response when someone whom you are talking to in English mutters?
8. What public figure do you consider to be an idiot? Explain.

Review Exercise

L.   Read the passage and fill in the blanks with the approptiate words from the chart on page 46. Then, answer the questions that follow.

Students in junior and senior high school are often given
(1) _____ tests in order to (2) _____ where their true
skills and interests lie. The idea behind the administration of such tests is
that when cognizant of each student's test results, school counselors will be
better able to advise him or her on which course to take and, eventually,
which career to prepare for. However, these tests have received some
criticism. Many educators and psychologists believe that the notion that a
school counselor can (3) _____ the path that a child's future will
take from such simple test results is idiotic. Critics feel that a young person
who is baffled by his or her own future would be better served by the
presentation of lucid explanations of various paths of study or career options.
Many educators, however, insist that, despite their (4) _____ ,
the tests are helpful. They point out that in the case of students with
behavioral problems, such as (5) _____ , counseling based on the
tests' results can often result in increased school attendance. They therefore
feel that continuing the use of the aptitude tests is a judicious decision.

1. What is the purpose of the aptitude tests? _____
_____

2. What do critics of the tests believe? _____
_____

3. What do the critics believe should be done for the children? _____
_____

4. What kind of behavioral problem can often be helped by counseling? _____
_____

Government (A)

WORDS FOR PRODUCTION

Word Form Chart

NOUN	VERB	ADJECTIVE	ADVERB
alignment	align	aligned	
ballot			
bully	bully		
crusade	crusade	crusading	
crusader			
	enfranchise	enfranchised	
exile	exile	exiled	
ideology		ideological	ideologically
	incite		
jurisdiction			
nomination	nominate		
overthrow	overthrown	overthrown	
persecution	persecute	persecuted	
prime minister			
	revoke	revocable	
		irrevocable	irrevocably
treason		treasonous	
tyrant		tyrannical	
tyranny			

Definitions and Examples

1. **align** [to put oneself on the side of or against a party or cause]

    The alignment of those countries with our enemies has made our situation worse.
    Most countries align themselves with a major power whose policies they agree with.
    Some countries consider themselves to be nonaligned.

2. **ballot** [a sheet of paper used to make a secret vote]

    It will take several hours to count the ballots and decide who has won.

3. **bully** [one who treats others abusively]

    The bigger boy was a bully and liked to fight the smaller boys.
    The more powerful countries are often accused of bullying the smaller countries into voicing agreement with their policies.

4. **crusade** [an enterprise undertaken with much enthusiasm, usually for some cause]

    The government has started a crusade against smoking.
    He has crusaded in favor of stricter speed limits ever since his daughter was killed by a speeding driver.
    The crusading women marched in the streets.
    She is a crusader against alcohol.

5. **enfranchise** [to allow the right to vote]

    Black people in the United States were enfranchised after the Civil War.
    Many of the recently enfranchised people are not yet registered to vote.

6. **exile** [forced removal from one's country]

    The rebels' leader was in exile in a neighboring country for ten years.
    The government exiled most of its critics.
    The exiled rebels are planning various acts of sabotage.

7. **ideology** [a systematic body of concepts, esp. about human life or culture]

    Their ideology opposes the private ownership of land.
    Many people in that society have ideological problems with the idea of children being raised in state centers rather than by their parents.
    Although they think that his idea is a practical one, they are ideologically opposed to it.

8. **incite** [to move to action]

    He was jailed on the charge of incitement to revolt.
    Her speech incited the workers to go out on strike.

9. **jurisdiction** [the power, right, or authority to apply the law]

> Murder is not within the jurisdiction of U.S. national courts because the laws against murder are state laws and the state courts have jurisdiction.

10. **nominate** [to propose as a candidate for election to office; to propose for a position of honor]

> She is campaigning now to win the nomination of her party.
> Each party nominated one candidate to run in the general election.
> The nominated candidates are going to debate each other on television next week.
> The nominating committee has chosen a new president to replace the one who resigned.

11. **overthrow** [to bring down; to defeat]

> The rebels are planning the overthrow of the king.
> They overthrew the government when government troops were used to collect more taxes.
> The overthrown government leaders are now living in exile.

12. **persecute** [to cause to suffer, esp. because of one's beliefs]

> The persecution of religious minorities has been common in the history of the world.
> The members of the opposition are being persecuted for their political beliefs.
> The persecuted opposition members are trying to leave the country.

13. **prime minister** [the chief executive of a parliamentary government]

> The British prime minister will meet with the American president today.

14. **revoke** [to take or call back]

> His license was revoked because he was found guilty of a hit-and-run accident in which a child was killed.
> The new law will be revocable in two years if it does not work out.
> Her resignation is irrevocable now; another person has already been hired to replace her.
> He is irrevocably committed to that ideology; nothing will change his mind.

15. **treason** [the offense of attempting to overthrow the government of one's own country]

> He was convicted of treason after his group tried to overthrow the government.
> Her sale of weapons to our enemies was a treasonous act.

16. **tyrant** [an absolute ruler unrestrained by law; a ruler who exercises absolute power oppressively]

> The people hate the king because he is such a tyrant.
> Her parents are quite tyrannical; she is never permitted out of the house alone.
> The tyrannical rule of that family over our country ended when its most important members were assassinated.

Exercises

A. Write **T** if the sentence is true and **F** if it is false.

_____ 1. People who are exiled are often imprisoned in the capital city of their country.

_____ 2. People like being bullied.

_____ 3. Being nominated is often the first step to getting elected.

_____ 4. The U.S. is always aligned with the U.S.S.R.

_____ 5. People want to be enfranchised.

_____ 6. Prime minister is a high-level position.

_____ 7. Ballots are used during elections.

_____ 8. People overthrow governments that they like.

_____ 9. Something that is irrevocable can be changed.

_____ 10. Treason is a serious crime.

B. Answer each question with a word from the word form chart on page 55.

1. Who hurts weaker people?
2. What are you in if you cannot live in your own country?
3. What do people want to do to tyrants?
4. Who may be the head of a government of a country?
5. What may be the first step in getting elected?
6. What is something people believe in?
7. What do people use to vote?
8. Who believes in something strongly and acts for it?
9. What are people who can vote?
10. What may a government do to people it does not like?
11. What might a person who hates his country commit?

C. Circle the word that is least related in meaning.

1. hurt   align   persecute
2. exile   nominate   choose
3. bully   ballot   vote
4. start   incite   enfranchise
5. overthrow   take back   revoke
6. bully   tyrant   crusader
7. incite   locate   align
8. jurisdiction   principles   ideology

D. Complete each analogy with a word from the word form chart on page 55.

1. tenets : religion :: _____ : political party
2. teacher : call on :: party : _____
3. bully : group of children :: _____ : country
4. expel : school :: _____ : country
5. paper : letter :: _____ : vote
6. set : fire :: _____ : riot

E. In the blanks, write the most appropriate words from the word form chart on page 55.

1. Many members of that minority group are leaving the country because they have been _____ .

2. The government currently has a(n) _____ to convince the people to buy more domestically produced products.

3. Small countries often feel that they must _____ themselves with one of the major powers.

4. The people will overthrow the king when they can no longer tolerate his

   _____ .

5. The government's _____ stops at the country's borders; it has no control over the actions of its neighbors.

6. He has lived in _____ since his act of treason was discovered.

7. Her party has to _____ her before she can officially run for that position.

8. Strong countries are sometimes accused of _____ their smaller neighbors and forcing them to go along with their decisions.

9. Those two men have quite different political _____ : one believes strongly in capitalism while the other is a communist.

10. Your driver's license may be _____ if you do not obey the traffic laws.

F.   Answer the following questions.

1. Have you ever crusaded for anything? Explain.
2. Does your country have a prime minister?
3. Has there ever been a period of tyranny in the history of your country? Explain.
4. Have certain groups in your country been persecuted? Explain.
5. What is the penalty for treason in your country?
6. Does the national court system in your country have jurisdiction over all crimes? Explain.
7. Which countries is your country aligned with?
8. What do you think is the best way for a child to handle a bully?
9. Have any famous people been exiled from your country? Explain.
10. Under what circumstances will a person's driver's license be revoked in your country?

WORDS FOR RECOGNITION

KEY WORD	SYNONYMS
consequence (n)	outgrowth, ramification
cut (v)	sever
incite (v)	abet, foment, instigate
overthrow (v)	subvert
prime minister (n)	premier
revoke (v)	abrogate, annul, nullify, rescind
right (n)	prerogative
scheme (n)	intrigue, plot
treason (n)	treachery

Example Sentences

consequence

An outgrowth of that situation is that some members of that group have been persecuted.
His treasonous acts will have a variety of ramifications.

cut

After that bombing incident, our government severed relations with that country, saying they were to blame.

incite

He was arrested for aiding and abetting a crime because he had supplied the weapons and helped plan the robbery.
That organization has been accused of fomenting revolution by encouraging the citizens to buy guns.
The problem was instigated by the refusal of people to stay home and indoors.

prime minister

The premier has called a meeting of his top ministers today.

revoke

The agreement was abrogated when neither side followed its guidelines.
The church annulled their marriage because they had never actually lived together.
The government plans to nullify its decision to drop its trade barriers if imports increase too rapidly.
Our permission to hold the parade has been rescinded because the police are afraid that there will be violence.

right

> It is the president's prerogative to make foreign policy decisions initially, but eventually he must convince the people that the policies are good ones.

scheme

> The government announced today the discovery of an intrigue to illegally sell weapons to our enemies.
> The plot to assassinate the prime minister failed because the gunman missed; the police have arrested four men and women who were involved.

treason

> The treachery of several people close to the president led to the downfall of the government.

Exercises

G. Circle the word that is least related in meaning.

1. abrogate   abet   rescind
2. subvert   foment   instigate
3. ramification   outgrowth   prerogative
4. treachery   intrigue   plot
5. sever   cut   abrogate
6. nullify   foment   annul
7. premier   president   prime minister

H. Write the key word for each set of words.

1. rescind   annul   _____
2. foment   abet   _____
3. intrigue   plot   _____
4. nullify   abrogate   _____
5. ramification   outgrowth   _____
6. abet   instigate   _____

I. Write the key word which corresponds to each italicized word.

1. Their attempt to *subvert* the administration failed. _____

2. It is the accused man's *prerogative* to consult a lawyer.

_____

3. Those two countries have *severed* relations. _____

4. Their *treachery* will not be forgotten. _____

5. The *premier* was assassinated last year. _____

6. The *ramifications* of this problem are not yet known. _____

7. The law passed last year was *nullified* last month. _____

8. She was accused of *fomenting* revolution. _____

9. He was involved in an *intrigue* to subvert the government.

_____

10. If she *instigates* any more trouble, she will be exiled. _____

J. Write **T** if the sentence is true and **F** if it is false.

_____ 1. The people involved in a plot have planned to do something.

_____ 2. Driving too fast is one outgrowth of traffic accidents.

_____ 3. You have a prerogative to do things which are against the law.

_____ 4. The subversion of a government will cause it to gain power.

_____ 5. Abetting a criminal is a crime.

_____ 6. A government usually punishes people who have committed treachery.

_____ 7. Countries may sever diplomatic relations if they have a major argument.

_____ 8. Good laws are usually rescinded.

K. Answer the following questions.

1. Think about one of your government's policies. What are some of its ramifications?
2. Has your government abrogated any of its laws? Explain.
3. Have there been any famous intrigues in the history of your country? Explain.
4. If a person is arrested in your country, what is it his prerogative to do?
5. Have there been any famous cases of treachery in your country? Explain.
6. Has your country recently severed ties with any other country? Explain.
7. Does your country have a premier?
8. Are marriages ever annulled in your country? Explain.

Nature (A)

WORDS FOR PRODUCTION

Word Form Chart

NOUN	VERB	ADJECTIVE	ADVERB
amphibian		amphibious	
		aquatic	
avalanche			
clearing			
ditch			
eeriness		eerie	eerily
fierceness		fierce	fiercely
hermit			
jeopardy	jeopardize		
ledge			
mist		misty	
predator		predatory	
prey	prey (on/upon)		
	pursue	pursuing	
		pursued	
remoteness		remote	remotely
	roam	roaming	
scavenger	scavenge		
	stalk	stalking	

Definitions and Examples

1. **amphibian** [an animal, machine, vehicle, etc. which can live or function both on land and in water]

   Frogs are amphibians.
   The enemy attacked with a large amphibious force which landed on the beach and then entered the town.

2. **aquatic** [growing, living in, or taking place in or on water]

   Water skiing is a popular aquatic sport in the United States.

3. **avalanche** [a large mass of snow, ice, earth, rock, or other material falling in swift motion down a mountainside or over a cliff]

   When it has snowed heavily in the mountains there is danger that avalanches will occur.

   {figurative}

   I was hit with such an avalanche of work this week that I could not handle it all.

4. **clearing** [an area of land cleared of wood and brush]

   We set up our tent in a small clearing in the woods.

5. **ditch** [a long, narrow hole dug in the earth, usually for defense, drainage, or irrigation]

   The men dug a ditch to carry the rainwater away from the cabin.

6. **eerie** [frightening because of strangeness or gloominess]

   The eeriness of that noise bothers me; I have never heard anything like it.
   The children were frightened by the eerie darkness in the old, abandoned house.
   A strange light glowed eerily in the northern sky.

7. **fierce** [violently hostile in temperament or nature]

   The fierceness of the storm knocked down power lines, leaving many homes without electricity.
   Their fierce attack left a large number of casualties on both sides.
   A mother cat in the wild will fiercely protect her offspring.

8. **hermit** [one who retires from society and lives alone]

   We saw an old hermit who lives in a cave in the mountains, but he ran away when he saw us.

9. **jeopardy** [exposure to or closeness to death, loss, or injury; danger]

   Her decision to climb that mountain alone has placed her life in jeopardy.
   Bad weather will jeopardize our plans to reach our destination by Tuesday.

10. **ledge** [a narrow, flat surface or shelf, especially one that extends out from a wall of rock]

> The bird was sitting on a narrow ledge, halfway up the side of the cliff.
> I have several plants on my outside window ledge.

11. **mist** [water in the form of particles floating or falling in the atmosphere, at or near the surface of the earth and approaching the form of rain]

> It was not really raining, but only misting as we waited for the bus.
> It is often misty and foggy near the lake in the early morning.

12. **predator** [an animal that lives by killing and consuming animals]

> The lion is a good example of a predator.

13. **prey (on/upon)** [to hunt, seize, and eat]

> Predators usually prey on smaller, weaker animals.
> The tiger hunted for two days before finding some suitable prey.

14. **pursue** [to follow in order to overtake, capture, kill, or defeat]

> Predators often pursue their prey for a long time before they are able to catch it.
> When she shot her rifle at the pursuing wolves, they ran away.
> The pursued rabbit had no hope of escape from the fox.

15. **remote** [far removed in space, time, or relation]

> The remoteness of that area makes emergency medical service there rather slow.
> He wants to live in a remote forested area, where there are no telephones or mail delivery.
> I am remotely related to that woman: her grandfather was my grandmother's nephew.

16. **roam** [to go from place to place without purpose or direction]

> Wild horses still roam the mountainous regions of the western portion of the United States.
> Roaming groups of thieves make that section of the country dangerous to travel in.

17. **scavenger** [an animal that feeds on waste]

> The desert scavengers will leave only the bones of that dead cow by morning.
> Some animals were scavenging in our trash can last night; the trash is scattered all over the place.

18. **stalk** [to pursue prey quietly and carefully]

> The cat silently stalked the feeding birds, hoping to catch one.
> The stalking hunters hid in the tall grass and watched their prey.

Exercises

A. Write **T** if the sentence is true and **F** if it is false.

_____ 1. Cats are amphibians.

_____ 2. Skiers fear avalanches.

_____ 3. Predators are usually weaker than their prey.

_____ 4. Hermits usually enjoy living in the city.

_____ 5. People want to be in jeopardy.

_____ 6. Aquatic plants can be seen in the ocean.

_____ 7. People tend to be afraid of eerie phenomena.

_____ 8. A predator often stalks its prey.

_____ 9. Mist most often occurs on sunny days.

_____ 10. Hermits usually live in remote areas.

_____ 11. A narrow ledge is a safe place to walk.

_____ 12. A ditch is a high area of land.

B. Answer each question with a word from the word form chart on page 64.

1. What is eaten by an animal?
2. What may a snowstorm cause?
3. What may be outside a window?
4. Who lives alone?
5. What is similar to light rain?
6. Where could you build a house in a forest?
7. What can water flow through?
8. What is a frog?
9. What kind of animals eat the remains of a dead animal?
10. What do predators do to their prey? (two answers)
11. How can you describe a lion? (two adjectives)

C. Circle the word that is least related in meaning.

1. hermit   person   amphibian
2. fierce   strange   eerie
3. endanger   pursue   jeopardize
4. rain   ditch   mist
5. roam   hunt   prey on
6. follow   pursue   scavenge
7. aquatic   fierce   strong
8. distant   eerie   remote

D. Complete each analogy with a word from the word form chart on page 64.

    1. athlete : competitive :: warrior : _____

    2. police : criminal :: predator : _____

    3. person : wander :: animal : _____

    4. water : flash flood :: snow : _____

    5. speak : whisper :: pursue : _____

    6. stalk : live animal :: _____ : dead animal

E. In the blanks, write the most appropriate words from the word form chart on page 64.

    1. Although the weather report had predicted a clear day, there was a light _____ falling as I got out of my car.

    2. She lives the life of a _____ up in the hills; she has not spoken to anyone in years.

    3. The _____ sports are most popular during the summer.

    4. There are too many rabbits in this region now because all of their _____ have been killed by man.

    5. A good hunter must be able to _____ his prey very quietly.

    6. Some people like to get away from civilization during their vacations and spend their time in _____ areas.

    7. You should avoid actions that place your life in _____ .

    8. We dug a _____ to carry the excess water away from our campground.

    9. _____ often follow behind predators and eat the parts of the prey that are left behind.

    10. The cattle are permitted to _____ all over the large ranch.

    11. Warriors usually try to look as _____ as possible when they go into battle.

F. Answer the following questions.

    1. Describe the most remote area of your country.
    2. Describe an eerie occurrence that you have witnessed.
    3. What is the largest predator in the wild in your country?
    4. Does your country have avalanches? Where? What causes them?
    5. Name some birds or animals in your country that are scavengers.
    6. Do your windows have ledges? If so, is anything on them?
    7. Are there any animals that used to roam freely in your country but no longer do? Explain.
    8. During what season of the year does mist occur in your country?

WORDS FOR RECOGNITION

KEY WORD	SYNONYMS
clearing (n)	glade
ditch (n)	gully, trench
cliff (n)	crag, escarpment
fierce (adj)	ferocious
jeopardize (v)	imperil
jump (v)	leap, spring
steep (adj)	precipitous, sheer
stream (n)	brook, creek
swamp (n)	bog, marsh, quagmire

Example Sentences

clearing

We had our picnic in a glade in the woods.

ditch

That gully next to the road fills with water when it rains.
In World War II the soldiers often fought from trenches.

cliff

There are several steep crags on that mountain.
They camped at the edge of an escarpment during their two-day climb up the
    mountain.

fierce

The animal became ferocious when it was cornered by the hunters and
    attacked them.

jeopardize

Our lives were imperiled by the sudden avalanche.

jump

The lion leaped at its prey and pulled it down.
The deer sprang away when it saw the bear.

steep

That cliff is so sheer that no one has ever climbed it.
The cliff at the side of the road fell away precipitiously.

stream

> A small brook runs through their backyard.
> He likes to fish in the creek on Saturdays.

swamp

> They are searching the bog for one of their cows; I hope it has not drowned.
> That marsh is a good place to go duck hunting in the fall.
> The truck got stuck as it was crossing the quagmire; the driver should have
>   stayed on the road.

Exercises

G. Circle the word that is least related in meaning.

1. imperil   spring   leap
2. gully   trench   glade
3. brook   quagmire   bog
4. precipitous   ferocious   sheer
5. creek   brook   gully
6. crag   escarpment   trench
7. clearing   creek   glade
8. spring   imperil   jeopardize
9. brook   bog   marsh

H. Write the key word for each set of words.

1. precipitous   sheer   _____
2. brook   creek   _____
3. trench   gully   _____
4. leap   spring   _____
5. quagmire   bog   _____

I. Write the key word that corresponds to each italicized word.

1. Do not do anything to *imperil* the success of this project.

_____

2. A lot of unusual vegetation grows in the *marsh.* _____

3. That *brook* is almost dry because of the recent lack of rain.

_____

4. It will be cool in the *glade.* _____

5. Some animals appear to be more *ferocious* than they really are.

_____

6. Do not go near the edge of the *escarpment.* _____

7. A shallow *gully* separates my property from hers. _____

8. He *leaped* and caught the ball. _____

9. It is easy to get lost in that *quagmire.* _____

10. They dug a *trench* to bury the wires in. _____

11. I want to reach the top of that *crag.* _____

12. The *creek* sometimes floods during heavy rains. _____

J. Write **T** if the sentence is true and **F** if it is false.

_____ **1.** The ground is wet in a bog.
_____ **2.** Wild animals can be ferocious.
_____ **3.** There can be many trees in a glade.
_____ **4.** You will imperil your life if you leap from an escarpment.
_____ **5.** A brook may run through a gully.
_____ **6.** Crags are not precipitous.
_____ **7.** You should spring into quagmires.
_____ **8.** The bottom of a trench in a marsh will be dry.
_____ **9.** The side of a crag is often sheer.

K. Answer the following questions.

1. How high can you leap into the air?
2. Which animal found in the wild in your country do you think is the most ferocious?
3. Describe a time when your life was imperiled.
4. Does your country have any marshes? If so, describe one.
5. Do you know of any sheer escarpments in your country? If so, describe one.
6. Describe a creek which you have seen.

Health (A)

WORDS FOR PRODUCTION

Word Form Chart

NOUN	VERB	ADJECTIVE	ADVERB
bandage	bandage	bandaged	
	choke	choking	
		chronic	chronically
coma		comatose	
dose			
dosage			
immunity	immunize	immune	
immunization			
nausea	nauseate	nauseated	
		nauseating	
numbness	numb	numb	numbly
		numbing	
ointment			
paralysis	paralyze	paralyzed	
		paralyzing	
plague	plague		
revival	revive	revived	
stretcher			

Definitions and Examples

1. **bandage** [a piece of fabric used to cover a wound]

   The nurse put a fresh bandage over the cut on the patient's leg.
   Wounds must be carefully bandaged to avoid infection.
   She could use her bandaged hand only awkwardly.

2. **choke** [to stop normal breathing by compressing or obstructing the windpipe or by poisoning the available air]

   He choked to death on a small chicken bone that caught in his throat.
   The choking firemen could not breathe because of the thick black smoke.

3. **chronic** [marked by long duration or frequent recurrence]

   That child misses a lot of school days because he has chronic colds every winter.
   Her employer dismissed her because she was chronically late.

4. **coma** [a state of deep unconsciousness caused by disease, injury, or poison]

   The accident victim is now in a coma and may not live.
   The comatose patient was not aware that her family was in the room with her.

5. **dose** [the measured quantity of a medicine to be taken at one time]

   The doctor told me to take one dose every four hours.
   The proper dosage for that medicine depends on the patient's body weight.

6. **immune** [having a high degree of resistance to a disease]

   Researchers try to find ways to increase people's immunity to disease.
   Many people are immune to some common diseases, like measles and mumps, because they have already had the disease once.

7. **immunize** [to make a person immune to a disease]

   They were foolish to enter the epidemic area without first being immunized.
   Proper immunizations are required to enter many countries.

8. **nausea** [a feeling that one does not want any food and may vomit]

   Many pregnant women experience nausea in the morning.
   The sight of that violence nauseated me.
   The nauseated passengers stayed in their cabins during much of the rough sea voyage.
   The nauseating smell of rotten food was strong in the dirty kitchen.

9. **numb** [without sensation, especially as a result of cold or anesthesia]

> The numbness of her hands and feet told her that she had been exposed to the severe cold for too long a time.
> The dentist gave me a shot to numb my mouth before he began to work.
> After the death of his wife, he felt so numb that he was unable even to cry.
> They knew that the numbing cold would kill them if they did not find shelter soon.

10. **ointment** [a cream for application to a wound on the skin]

> The doctor gave her an ointment to put on the burn twice a day.

11. **paralysis** [complete or partial loss of a function, especially when involving the loss of motion or sensation in a part of the body]

> He suffered partial paralysis of the left side of his body as a result of the damage to his brain in the accident.
> The paralyzed little girl was unable to walk.
> He was struck with a paralyzing pain and fell to the ground.

12. **plague** [an epidemic disease causing a high rate of death]

> A plague named the "Black Death" killed almost half of the population of Europe during the thirteenth century.

> {figurative}

> This project has been plagued with problems; we may never finish it.

13. **revive** [to return to consciousness or life]

> The revival of that section of the city is due to the efforts of the new mayor.
> The doctor attempted to revive the patient but failed. He was the third fatality of that accident.
> The revived man thanked the doctor for saving his life.

14. **stretcher** [a device (usually of canvas) for carrying a dead, injured, or sick person]

> The victims of the crash were carried to the waiting ambulances by stretcher.

Exercises

A. Write **T** if the sentence is true and **F** if it is false.

_____ **1.** People who are in comas sometimes revive and sometimes die.

_____ **2.** A nurse may put a stretcher on a wound.

_____ **3.** If a person is choking, he or she is having trouble breathing.

_____ **4.** If you are immune to a disease, you will not catch that disease.

_____ **5.** Being numb hurts a lot.

_____ **6.** To take care of a wound, first you put on a bandage, and then you put on an ointment.

_____ **7.** If you are chronically sick, then you are rarely sick.

_____ **8.** You should be careful to take the correct dosage of any medicine.

_____ **9.** Doctors use plagues to cure patients' nausea.

B. Answer each question with a word from the word form chart on page 72.

1. What are you suffering from if you cannot move your legs?
2. What two things can be put on a cut?
3. What may happen if something gets caught in your throat?
4. What are you in if you cannot be awakened?
5. What feeling makes you not want to eat?
6. What occurs if you put ice on an injury?
7. What is used to carry injured people?
8. What type of sickness kills many people?
9. What do doctors try to do to unconscious people?

C. Circle the word or phrase that is least related in meaning.

1. amount   numbness   dosage
2. immune   nauseated   sick
3. ointment   medicine   paralysis
4. continual   chronic   revived
5. chronic   sensationless   numb
6. covered   nauseated   bandaged
7. plagued by   revived by   bothered by

D. In the blanks, write the most appropriate words from the word form chart on page 72.

1. The child fell into the water, and we thought that he had drowned, but the rescue workers _____ him.

2. It took two strong people to carry the _____ with the old man's body on it.

3. You should keep a(n) _____ on that cut until it heals.

4. The motion of the ship made me feel _____ .

5. Do not try to swallow your food without chewing it first, or you will

   _____ .

6. The doctor said that applying this _____ to the burn on your hand will make it feel better.

7. His legs became _____ when his backbone was broken.

8. She needs good health insurance coverage because she is

   _____ sick and has many medical bills to pay.

9. Modern medical research has eliminated many of the circumstances that

   lead to _____ .

10. The little girl has been in a(n) _____ since the accident.

E. Answer the following questions.

1. Explain some ways to revive a person who has fainted.
2. What should you do if a person is choking on a piece of food?
3. How do you know what the proper dosage of a medicine is?
4. Do you have any chronic medical problems? Explain.
5. When was the most recent plague in your country?
6. Have you ever been cold enough to feel numb? Explain.
7. Does traveling by car make you feel nauseated? By boat?
8. What diseases are you immune to? Why?

WORDS FOR RECOGNITION

KEY WORD	SYNONYMS
bandage (n)	dressing
beginning (n)	onset
dangerous (n)	perilous
die (v)	expire, pass away, pass on
disease (n)	disorder, malady
dizziness (n)	vertigo
handicapped (adj)	crippled, disabled, lame
nauseated (adj)	queasy
pill (n)	capsule, tablet
pretend (v)	feign
recover (v)	recuperate
sleepy (adj)	drowsy
thin (adj) (negative)	emaciated, gaunt, skinny

Example Sentences

bandage

The nurse put a fresh dressing on his wound this morning.

beginning

The doctor said that the onset of the disease is gradual.

dangerous

Some immunizations are themselves dangerous, but it is usually much more perilous to not be immunized.

die

The patient expired at exactly one o'clock.
My grandfather passed away last year.
When she passes on, there will be no members of that family left alive.

disease

Some disorders of the liver are caused by drinking too much alcohol.
She is suffering from an unidentified malady.

dizziness

This ear infection is giving me vertigo.

handicapped

He is crippled and cannot walk.
She is disabled but has a specially engineered automobile so that she can drive.
She has been lame since her leg was broken and did not heal correctly.

nauseated

I think that I had better lie down; I feel queasy.

pill

These capsules contain a strong pain medicine.
He takes tablets before each meal to help settle his stomach.

pretend

The doctors think that nothing is wrong with her and that she is only feigning
    an illness.

recover

He will have to spend several weeks recuperating from that surgical
    procedure.

sleepy

Since the medicine will make you feel drowsy, you should not drive your car
    after taking it.

thin

Eight months of illness have left her emaciated.
My grandmother is a tall, gaunt woman.
He is too skinny; he should try to put on some weight.

Exercises

F.   Circle the word or phrase that is least related in meaning.

1. lame   crippled   queasy
2. pass on   feign   expire
3. gaunt   drowsy   emaciated
4. vertigo   dressing   bandage
5. disabled   perilous   crippled
6. onset   tablet   capsule
7. get better   recuperate   feign
8. pretend   pass away   expire
9. malady   onset   disorder

G. Write the key word for each set of words.

1. skinny   gaunt   _____

2. pass away   pass on   _____

3. capsule   tablet   _____

4. disabled   lame   _____

5. disorder   malady   _____

6. expire   pass away   _____

7. lame   crippled   _____

8. emaciated   gaunt   _____

H. Write the key word that corresponds to each italicized word.

1. I always feel *drowsy* by ten o'clock. _____

2. He cannot get out of bed because of *vertigo*. _____

3. I need some fresh air; I feel *queasy*. _____

4. He is *feigning* those symptoms. _____

5. The *onset* of the disease occurred last year. _____

6. That course of treatment may be *perilous*. _____

7. She is *recuperating* nicely. _____

8. That *dressing* needs to be changed. _____

9. He has become *emaciated*. _____

10. That *disorder* is very serious. _____

11. She took two small *tablets*. _____

12. He *passed away* suddenly. _____

I. Choose all the possible antonyms for each word from the group of words and phrases below and write them on the line. The antonyms should be the same part of speech as the cue word.

1. get worse _____

2. awake _____

3. live _____

4. ending _____

5. fat _____

6. safe _____

skinny	pass on	onset
recuperate	drowsy	emaciated
perilous	expire	gaunt
pass away		

J. Write **T** if the sentence is true and **F** if it is false.

_____ **1.** Capsules should be as large as possible.

_____ **2.** Most people pass on before the onset of a malady.

_____ **3.** People put on a dressing when they feel queasy.

_____ **4.** A person with vertigo may fall down easily.

_____ **5.** People often expire from feigned disorders.

_____ **6.** An emaciated person needs to gain weight.

_____ **7.** People have trouble working when they are drowsy.

_____ **8.** People should avoid perilous activities.

_____ **9.** People who have passed away can recuperate.

K. Answer the following questions.

1. Describe a time when you felt that your life was in peril.
2. What do you do to stay awake when you feel drowsy?
3. Choose a disease that you are familiar with and describe the typical onset of the symptoms.
4. Describe the traditional events in your country when a member of the family passes away.
5. Name a famous person who is skinny.
6. Are there special facilities in your country for disabled people? Describe them.
7. What do you do to feel better if you begin to feel queasy?
8. Have you ever experienced vertigo? What was the cause?
9. Do you have difficulty swallowing capsules? How do you manage to take them when you need to?

Money

WORDS FOR PRODUCTION

Word Form Chart

NOUN	VERB	ADJECTIVE
auction	auction off	auctioned
bankruptcy	bankrupt	bankrupt
deficit		
dividend		
foreclosure	foreclose	
forfeiture	forfeit	forfeited
outlay	outlay	
		overdue
pawnshop	pawn	pawned
pawnbroker		
pawn ticket		
revenue		
share		
shareholder		
solvency		solvent
insolvency		insolvent
speculation	speculate	
speculator		
thrift		thrifty
thriftiness		
voucher	vouch for	

Definitions and Examples

1. **auction** [a public sale of property to whomever offers the highest price]

    > They held an auction and sold all of their possessions in one day.
    > If that store goes out of business, all of its goods will be auctioned off.
    > The auctioned goods brought in over five thousand dollars.

2. **bankrupt** [unable to pay one's debts when they are due]

    > That company has filed for bankruptcy with the court; if it owes you money, you may not be paid.
    > One of the company officials bankrupted the company by embezzling most of its funds.
    > Bankrupt stores often sell off their remaining goods very cheaply.
    > Many businesses may go bankrupt because of the new restrictions on exports.

3. **deficit** [an excess of spending compared to income]

    > Many members of parliament do not approve of the proposed budget because it will result in a deficit.

4. **dividend** [a sum or fund to be divided and distributed]

    > That company has paid large dividends to its investors for the past three years.

5. **foreclosure** [a legal procedure that permits a credit institution, such as a bank, to take possession of something bought on credit (usually a property or building) because credit payments were not adequately made]

    > There have been several foreclosures on farms this year because of the lack of rain.
    > If the bank forecloses on our loan, it will auction off our house.

6. **forfeit** [to lose, or lose the right to, by some error, offense, or crime]

    > The rental contract requires forfeiture of our deposit if the car is not in good condition when we return it.
    > He forfeited his right to vacation time by coming in late on so many days.
    > The forfeited money will be turned over to the government.

7. **outlay** [the amount of money spent]

    > We hope that our profits will cover our initial outlay within the first six months.
    > The company will outlay enough money to put a deposit on the equipment.

8. **overdue** [unpaid when due; delayed beyond an appointed time]

    > The telephone bill is already a week overdue; I should have paid it last Wednesday.

9. **pawn** [to deposit an item as security for a debt]

> When I needed money, I went into the local pawnshop and pawned my
> grandfather's watch.
> The pawned articles can be reclaimed by presenting the pawn ticket to
> the pawnbroker and paying him back the borrowed money.

10. **revenue** [the total income produced by a given source]

> The government hopes that tax revenues will rise as the incomes of the
> people rise.

11. **share** [any of the equal portions into which property or invested capital is
divided]

> My father owns five hundred shares of stock in that company.
> All of the shareholders are invited to a meeting twice a year to vote on
> company policies.

12. **solvent** [able to pay all legal debts]

> The solvency of that company is in question; some people think that it
> will go bankrupt soon.
> They will have to cut the workers' wages in order to stay solvent.
> The shareholders are worried about the rumors concerning the insolvency
> of the company.
> If they are really insolvent, they will be forced to declare bankruptcy.

13. **speculate** [to buy or sell in expectation of profiting from changes in the
market]

> Buying those shares of that new company was pure speculation on his
> part; he had no way of knowing that their value would increase so
> much.
> You could lose a lot of money if you speculate without knowing exactly
> how the stock market works.
> Her actions in buying and selling that stock so quickly were those of a
> speculator.

14. **thrifty** [practicing economy and good management]

> You can save a lot of money through thrift.
> She is very thrifty; she rarely wastes anything.
> We admired their thriftiness in reusing all of the paper bags.

15. **vouch for** [to give a guarantee]

> My parents had to vouch for my car loan because my income is low.
> I can vouch for his honesty; he has worked for me for ten years.

16. **voucher** [a document record of a business deal]

> Be sure to turn in your vouchers when you return from each business
> trip.

Exercises

A. Write **T** if the sentence is true and **F** if it is false.

_____ 1. A business that goes bankrupt is insolvent.

_____ 2. People want to get dividends.

_____ 3. An auction is a private sale.

_____ 4. A thrifty person saves money.

_____ 5. If you spend too much, you will have a deficit.

_____ 6. Wealthy people often pawn their possessions.

_____ 7. You should not vouch for a person unless you trust him.

_____ 8. If you start a business, you want a large outlay.

_____ 9. When you forfeit something, you lose it.

_____ 10. Each shareholder of a company owns part of it.

B. Answer each question with a word from the word form chart on page 81.

1. What shows proof of a business deal? _voucher?_

2. What kind of a sale does not have fixed prices? _auction_

3. Where can you obtain money in exchange for one of your possessions? _pawn shop_

4. What will the bank do if you do not make your loan payments on time? _foreclose_

5. Who buys and sells in hopes of making a profit? _speculator_

6. What do shareholders own? _shares_

7. What does a government have if it spends more than it takes in? _deficit_

8. What are taxes for the government? _revenue_

9. What is a bill that you should have paid by yesterday but did not pay? _overdue_

10. What are you if you cannot pay your bills? (two answers) _bankrupt/insolvent_

C. Circle the word or phrase that is least related in meaning.

1. outlay   late   overdue

2. forfeit   give up   speculate

3. bankrupt   insolvent   thrifty

4. foreclose   guarantee   vouch for

5. share   deficit   portion

6. pawned   thrifty   economical

7. sale   auction   voucher

D. In the blanks, write the most appropriate words from the word form chart on page 81.

1. She is known for her _____ because she gets by on very little money each month.

2. She _____ some of her jewelry in order to get enough money for her ticket.

3. As a(n) _____ in this company, you can participate in a small way in the running of the company.

4. He is constantly buying and selling shares of various companies because he is a(n) _____ .

5. The bank will _____ on that property soon if they do not make some payments on their loan.

6. I can _____ her honesty; she has worked in our bank for over twenty years and we trust her completely.

7. Many people go to _____ to get bargains on old furniture.

8. If your phone bill is _____ , the phone company may disconnect your service.

9. Our _____ for this project was so large that we will have to take in a lot of money before we will be able to show a profit.

10. That company often pays large _____ to its shareholders.

E. Answer the following questions.

1. Are banks in your country permitted to foreclose on overdue loans? Explain.
2. Have you ever pawned anything? If so, explain.
3. Do you consider yourself to be a thrifty person? Why or why not?
4. Does your country have a budget deficit? Why or why not?
5. Have you ever bought anything at an auction? If so, explain.
6. Which of your friends or relatives would you be willing to vouch for?
7. Does your country have laws concerning bankruptcy proceedings? If so, explain.

WORDS FOR RECOGNITION

KEY WORD	SYNONYMS
bankrupt (adj)	broke (colloq.)
deal (n)	transaction
greed (n)	avarice
jewel (n)	gem
pay (v)	defray
poor (adj)	indigent, impoverished, needy
save (v)	put aside, put away
thrifty (adj)	frugal
trade (v)	barter, swap (colloq.)

Example Sentences

bankrupt

She went broke when her business failed.

deal

He is busy working on an important business transaction right now.

greed

Pure avarice led him to embezzle the money.

jewel

She wore a necklace with several gems in it.

pay

The company will defray the costs of your trip.

poor

Some indigent people in this city are living in the streets.
The family was left impoverished when the father committed suicide.
Needy people can receive help from the government.

save

When you have a good job, you should put aside money for times when
finding work may be difficult.
I put away enough money over the past year to take off work for two months
and travel.

thrifty

Her lifestyle is very frugal; she rarely spends much money.

trade

Long ago, people often bartered for the things that they needed; nowadays, most people use cash or credit.

The little boy swapped his bike for a new baseball glove.

Exercises

F. Circle the word or phrase that is least related in meaning.

1. put on   put away   put aside
2. greed   avarice   gem
3. broke   frugal   bankrupt
4. needy   defray   indigent
5. put aside   swap   barter
6. deal   transaction   gem
7. impoverished   indigent   frugal

G. Write the key word for each set of words.

1. needy   impoverished   _____
2. swap   barter   _____
3. put aside   put away   _____
4. indigent   impoverished   _____

H. Write the key word that corresponds to each italicized word.

1. That *gem* is worth a lot of money. _____
2. The *transaction* was a successful one for us. _____
3. The company went *broke.* _____
4. His *avarice* is such that he is never satisfied. _____
5. Being *frugal* has its rewards. _____
6. My insurance will *defray* the cost of a rental car. _____
7. The fund will help the *needy.* _____
8. The people in that community *barter* for the goods they need. _____
9. How much have you *put aside?* _____
10. She has been *impoverished* for several years. _____

I.   Write **T** if the sentence is true and **F** if it is false.

      ____ **1.** Indigent people often do not have good clothing.

      ____ **2.** You need money to barter.

      ____ **3.** People like to be broke.

      ____ **4.** Robbers will steal gems if they can.

      ____ **5.** Thrifty people put aside money for the future.

      ____ **6.** Bankers try to avoid financial transactions.

      ____ **7.** Avaricious people usually give away a lot of money.

      ____ **8.** A frugal person is usually careful about spending money.

J.   Answer the following questions.

1. Is anyone defraying the cost of your education for you? If so, who?

2. Are there government programs to aid the indigent in your country? Explain.

3. Who is the most frugal person that you know?

4. Do you find it easy to put away money? Why or why not?

5. Which type of gem do you feel is the most beautiful? Do certain gems traditionally have particular significance in your country? Explain.

6. What types of things are bartered in your country?

7. Name someone who you think suffers from avarice.

8. Where do the most needy people in your town or city live?

Review Exercise

K. Read the passage and fill in the blanks with the appropriate words from the word form chart on page 81.

My first business went (1) _____ after only two years. I just was not able to do enough business to avoid insolvency. It was a very sad day in my life when the bank (2) _____ on my mortgage and ordered me to (3) _____ all of my business assets in order to pay as much of the debt as I could.

While I am not an anxious person, I was determined that I would never go broke again. I wanted to open another business as soon as possible, but I knew it would take some time for me to put aside enough money for the initial (4) _____ of opening a new business.

Finally I decided that this time I could not do it alone; instead, I would find partners to invest in my next business venture. Of course, it was difficult to find investors who could be convinced to (5) _____ on my chance for success. However, eventually I found several people who were willing to gamble on my dreams of success. They became (6) _____ in the company in the hope of receiving large (7) _____ when the business began to make a profit. I would rather have begun the company by myself, but it was necessary to (8) _____ some of the control of the business in order to get enough capital to get it started.

Clothing

WORDS FOR PRODUCTION

Word Form Chart

NOUN	VERB	ADJECTIVE	ADVERB
bleach	bleach	bleached	
		bleaching	
crease	crease	creased	
cuff			
fastener	fasten	fastened	
heel			
hem	hem	hemmed	
lining	line	lined	
mannequin			
		ostentatious	ostentatiously
pleat	pleat	pleated	
rack			
rinse	rinse	rinsed	
seam			
seamstress			
sole			
tailor	tailor	tailored	
zipper	zip		

Definitions and Examples

1. **bleach** [to remove color or stains from]

    I put bleach in with my white clothing in the wash.
    If you bleach that white tablecloth, the wine stain may come out.
    She has bleached blond hair.
    That bleaching solution is very strong; it may damage your clothes.

2. **crease** [a line or mark made by folding or pressing]

    His pants had a neat crease down the front of each leg.
    Be careful not to crease your dress when you put it in the suitcase.
    These creased shirts need to be ironed.

3. **cuff** (a) [something encircling the wrist]

    The cuffs of my shirts always get dirty when I write in pencil.

    (b) [the turned-up bottom of a pants leg]

    Those pants have one-inch cuffs.

4. **fasten** [to attach; to secure against opening]

    There were two types of buttons serving as fasteners on his coat.
    Please fasten the gate on your way out.
    The fastened buttons on her coat were gold.

5. **heel** [the back of the foot, behind the ankle; the back, usually elevated portion of a shoe]

    Her shoes had high heels and looked difficult to walk in.

6. **hem** [an edge of a cloth article doubled back and sewed down]

    The hem on that skirt is two inches deep, so it can be lengthened.
    I will have to hem these new pants before I can wear them.
    The hemmed dress fit her perfectly.

7. **line** [to cover the inner surface of something (especially clothing)]

    The lining of my winter coat is wool.
    I plan to line this skirt that I am making.
    The lined jacket is more expensive than this unlined one.

8. **mannequin** [a form representing the human figure, used especially for displaying clothes]

    The mannequin in the store window was wearing a red dress.

9. **ostentatious** [done in a way that is showing off; calling attention to itself]

   The diamonds sewn on that jacket are quite ostentatious.
   He always dresses ostentatiously, as if he is trying to impress everyone.

10. **pleat** [a fold in cloth made by doubling the material over on itself]

    That style shirt has a pleat down the back.
    She wore a pleated skirt.

11. **rack** [a device upon which things (especially clothing) can be hung]

    The store had two racks of coats on sale.

12. **rinse** [to clean by clear water, especially to clean out the soap used in washing]

    He rinsed the soap out of the sweater in the sink.

13. **seam** (a) [the joining of two pieces (usually of cloth) by sewing (usually near the edge)]

    This seam needs to be sewn together again; it is coming apart.

    (b) **seamstress** [a woman whose occupation is sewing]

    I need to take these skirts to the seamstress to have the hems let down.

14. **sole** [the undersurface of a foot or shoe]

    The soles of my shoes are always the first part to wear out.

15. **tailor** (a) [one whose occupation is making or altering clothes]

    That suit was made by a local tailor.

    (b) [to make or alter clothes]

    That coat was tailored very nicely.

16. **zipper** [a fastener consisting of two rows of metal or plastic teeth, which are pulled together by a sliding piece]

    That skirt has a zipper in the back.
    Zip up your coat before you go out; it is cold out there.

Exercises

A. Write **T** if the sentence is true and **F** if it is false.

_____ 1. Zippers are usually made of wood.

_____ 2. Mannequins look like people.

_____ 3. Bleach is usually used on white clothing.

_____ 4. If an article of clothing is ostentatious, it will not get people's attention.

_____ 5. Winter coats are not usually lined.

_____ 6. You rinse something after washing it with soap.

_____ 7. Clothing stores display their merchandise on racks.

_____ 8. A pleated skirt needs to be ironed to get rid of the pleats.

B. Answer each question with a word from the word form chart on page 90.

1. What may be at the end of the leg of a pair of pants?
2. What do you change if you want to change the length of a skirt?
3. Who does alterations on clothing? (two answers)
4. How can you get soap off of something?
5. What is a zipper an example of?
6. On what do you find clothes in a store?
7. What makes clothes white?
8. What is inside your clothes?
9. What kind of clothing do you not want to wear?
10. What often happens to clothing that is packed?

C. Circle the word that is least related in meaning.

1.	hem	bleach	dye
2.	sole	crease	bottom
3.	pleat	doll	mannequin
4.	close	fasten	bleach
5.	rinse	line	wash
6.	tailor	cuff	seamstress
7.	rack	button	zipper

D. Complete each analogy with a word from the word form chart on page 90.

1. fold : paper :: _____ : cloth
2. behavior : show off :: clothing : be _____
3. book : shelf :: dress : _____
4. cotton : material :: _____ : fastener
5. cover : outside :: _____ : inside
6. actor : actress :: _____ : seamstress
7. palm : hand :: _____ : foot
8. soap : dirt :: _____ : color

E. In the blanks, write the most appropriate words from the word form chart on page 90.

1. There will be a lot of stress on those _____ , so sew them with heavy thread.

2. Most _____ are tall and thin so that the clothing will look good on them.

3. You should check the label in each article of clothing to make sure that it is safe to _____ it.

4. You did not _____ this thoroughly; there is still soap in it.

5. Those _____ will come out when you iron it.

6. I got chewing gum on the _____ of my shoe.

7. Her dress was so _____ that everyone in the room was staring at it.

8. My winter jacket needs a new _____ ; the old one is broken and will not move.

9. The _____ altered this suit for me, and he did a very nice job.

10. That store has so many clothes on sale that they do not have enough _____ to put them on.

F. Answer the following questions.

1. Do you prefer that stores have separate racks for different sizes, or for different colors or styles?
2. How do you avoid getting creases in your clothing?
3. Do you like pants with cuffs?
4. Have you taken any of your clothing to a tailor or seamstress recently? For what purpose?
5. Do you prefer rubber or leather soles on your shoes? Why?
6. Describe a person whom you saw recently who was dressed ostentatiously.

WORDS FOR RECOGNITION

KEY WORD	SYNONYMS
beautiful (adj)	gorgeous, stunning
dull (adj)	drab
clean (v)	scour, scrub
clothing (n)	apparel, attire
crease (v)	crumple
examine (v)	scrutinize
flashy (adj)	garish, gaudy
foam (n)	suds
hand-me-down (n)	castoff
preference (n)	penchant, predilection, propensity
ripped (adj)	tattered
sew (v)	stitch (up)
ugly (adj)	hideous
undress (v)	disrobe, strip

Example Sentences

beautiful

> The dress in the shop window looked gorgeous.
> She looked stunning in her new dress.

dull

> He wears a drab gray suit to work every day.

clean

> The sink is dirty; it needs to be scoured.
> She scrubbed the spot on her skirt, but it would not come out.

clothing

> That store sells men's apparel.
> Formal attire was required at that wedding.

crease

> His suit looked crumpled after the long trip.

examine

> She carefully scrutinized the blouse before she took it to the cash register.

flashy

That red suit is too garish; I would not wear it in public.
She prefers quiet-colored clothes that are not at all gaudy.

foam

The amount of suds shows how much soap is in the water.

hand-me-down

They are so poor that the children only wear castoffs from neighbors' children.

preference

He has a penchant for red ties; he wears one almost every day.
Her predilection for fur coats is well known; people say that she has five of
    them.
I dislike his propensity to talk constantly.

ripped

Her tattered coat was obviously old.

sew

I need to stitch that rip in my shirt.

ugly

That color is hideous. Why would anyone buy that dress?

undress

The nurse instructed me to disrobe.
The members of the team stripped and went into the shower room.

Exercises

G. Circle the word that is least related in meaning.

1. tattered   hideous   ugly
2. drab   dirty   dull
3. attire   stitch   apparel
4. crumple   castoff   crease
5. beautiful   stunning   garish
6. penchant   foam   suds
7. scrub   stitch   sew
8. tattered   ripped   gaudy

H. Write the key word for each set of words.

1. propensity   predilection   _____
2. scrub   scour   _____
3. attire   apparel   _____
4. garish   gaudy   _____
5. strip   disrobe   _____
6. penchant   propensity   _____

I. Write the key word that corresponds to each italicized word.

1. No one will buy that _hideous_ dress. _____
2. Be sure that there are lots of _suds_ in the washer. _____
3. The child was wearing _castoffs._ _____
4. His suit was _crumpled._ _____
5. The _tattered_ clothing was old. _____
6. He _scrutinized_ his image in the mirror. _____
7. I can _stitch_ that _up_ quickly. _____
8. That color is _garish._ _____
9. Please _scour_ those pans. _____
10. Her _attire_ was appropriate for the party. _____
11. Her new hairstyle is _stunning._ _____
12. He _stripped._ _____

J. Choose all the possible antonyms for each word from the group of words below and write them on the line. The antonyms should be the same part of speech as the cue word.

1. beautiful _____
2. get dirty _____
3. ugly _____
4. dress (v) _____
5. quiet _____

stunning	drab	scrub	garish
scour	strip	crumple	disrobe
gaudy		suds	hideous

K. Write **T** if the sentence is true and **F** if it is false.

_____ 1. A dirty bathtub needs to be scoured.

_____ 2. People strip before they take a bath.

_____ 3. Castoffs are usually stunning.

_____ 4. Drab clothes are often gaudy.

_____ 5. When you scrutinize something, you look at it carefully.

_____ 6. You should be careful to avoid producing suds while you are washing something.

_____ 7. People want their clothing to be crumpled.

_____ 8. Something that is stunning is attractive.

_____ 9. One should be careful about one's attire for a job interview.

_____ 10. Tattered clothing is in good condition.

L. Answer the following questions.

1. Where do you usually buy most of your apparel?
2. Did you wear castoffs when you were a child? Whose? Did you like them?
3. Is it ever the custom to wear dark, drab clothing in your country? When?
4. Do you scrutinize an article of clothing before you buy it? Why?
5. What attire is appropriate for a wedding in your country?
6. What kind of clothing do you have a penchant for?
7. What do you have a propensity to do when you are angry?
8. Can you stitch a straight seam?
9. Which actress do you think is stunning?

Review Exercise

M. Choose the appropriate words from the charts on pages 90 and 95 to answer the following questions.

1. Which words are related to the making of clothing?

   (n) _____   (n) _____

   (n) _____

2. Which words are related to the washing of clothing?

   (n) _____   (v) _____

   (n) _____

   (v) _____   (v) _____

3. Which adjectives are used to favorably describe clothing?

   _____   _____

4. Which adjectives are used to negatively describe clothing?

   _____   _____   _____

   _____   _____

5. Which nouns may refer to parts of a skirt?

   _____   _____   _____

   _____   _____

Media

WORDS FOR PRODUCTION

Word Form Chart

NOUN	VERB	ADJECTIVE	ADVERB
absurdity		absurd	absurdly
		caustic	caustically
blurriness	blur	blurry	
deletion	delete	deleted	
distortion	distort	distorted	
facade			
hint	hint		
hoax			
incisiveness		incisive	incisively
		lurid	
		painstaking	painstakingly
		sensational	sensationally
stuttering	stutter	stuttering	
stutterer			
vehemence		vehement	vehemently

Definitions and Examples

1. **absurd** [ridiculously unreasonable; meaningless]

   The absurdity of the reporter's description made us laugh.
   Many people find the idea of the government's paying farmers not to
     plant crops absurd.

2. **caustic** (a) [capable of destroying or eating away by chemical action]

> That substance is caustic and will eat its way out of any nonglass container.

(b) [biting; cutting]

> She can be quite caustic when she disagrees with you.
> He caustically listed my failures.

3. **blurry** [indistinct; difficult to read]

> The newspaper was old, and the blurriness of the print made it difficult to read.
> The tears in my eyes blurred the words on the page as I read the sad story.
> His head injury will cause him to have blurry vision for a few days.

4. **delete** [eliminate; take out]

> The deletion by his editor of several key paragraphs angered the reporter.
> I will have to delete about half of this in order to meet the maximum length requirement.
> The deleted information was not central to the topic of the article.

5. **distort** [to change from the real meaning or proportion]

> The public will not tolerate any distortion of the news by the government.
> He distorted the truth by telling them only half of the story.
> They did not believe her distorted version of the story.

6. **facade** (a) [a face, especially of a building]

> The facade of the old building was black with dirt.

(b) [a false, superficial, or artificial appearance or effect]

> His facade is one of concern for our problem, but underneath he does not really care at all.

7. **hint** [an indirect suggestion]

> The article gave only a hint of the underlying problem.
> She hinted that she may quit her job soon.

8. **hoax** [an act intended to trick]

> The whole business deal was a hoax; they never intended to complete the transaction. They only wanted to take our attention away from their true intentions.

9. **incisive** [impressively direct]

> We admired her incisiveness in dealing with the troublemakers; she went straight to their leader and demanded an end to their actions.
> His incisive action ended the strife immediately.
> She incisively decided to deal directly with the opposition leader.

10. **lurid** [causing horror]

> The article contained such lurid pictures that I could not stand to look at them.

11. **painstaking** [using diligent care and effort; attending to detail]

> His efforts to uncover the whole story were painstaking and lasted for weeks.
> She painstakingly examined all of the evidence, even that which seemed to be of no value.

12. **sensational** [intended to cause quick and superficial interest, curiosity, or emotional reaction]

> The pictures and stories in that paper are far too sensational; they sacrifice accuracy for whatever they feel will attract readers.
> This story was written too sensationally; the headline draws one's attention, but it does not dig deeply into the issue.

13. **stutter** [to speak with involuntary blocking of speech]

> Many children go through a phase of stuttering when they try to speak rapidly.
> An adult who stutters may be helped by special training.
> The stuttering boy was very difficult to follow.
> I have been a stutterer since I was a child, so I do not enjoy speaking in front of groups of people.

14. **vehement** [very emotional]

> We were shocked by his vehemence on the issue.
> She was vehement in her opposition to the plan.
> They vehemently denied that they had been responsible for the breakdown.

Exercises

A. Write **T** if the sentence is true and **F** if it is false.

_F_ 1. People want to stutter.

_F_ 2. Editors delete information that they want to include.

_T_ 3. A hoax may fool people.

_T_ 4. People are vehement about things they feel strongly about.

_T_ 5. Blurry print is difficult to read.

_F_ 6. People usually work painstakingly when they do not care about their job.

_T_ 7. News reporters should try to report the facts.

_I_ **8.** When someone hints, he or she is not speaking incisively.

_I_ **9.** A public facade may hide a private life.

_I_ **10.** People are attracted to sensational stories.

_I_ **11.** A caustic remark could hurt someone's feelings.

_F_ **12.** Small children should watch lurid movies.

B. Answer each question with a word from the word form chart on page 100.

1. What should you do to a sentence that is unrelated to the paragraph it is in? _delete it_
2. What is something that is ridiculous? _absurd (ludicrous?)_
3. What kind of comment may hurt someone? _caustic_
4. What can you do when you do not want to state your opinion directly? _hint_
5. What is a speech problem? _stutter_
6. What may fool people? _hoax_
7. How can you describe news that is not accurate? _distortion_
8. How do bosses want their employees to work? _painstakingly_
9. What is visible on the outside, but may cover the truth inside? _facade_
10. How can you describe questions that are clear and direct? _incisive_

C. Circle the word or phrase that is least related in meaning.

1. incisive   vehement   emotional

2. suggest   delete   hint

3. painstaking   blurry   diligent

4. facade   exterior   interior

5. change   distort   stutter

6. absurd   incisive   direct

7. trick   facade   hoax

8. vehement   horrible   lurid

D. Complete each analogy with a word from the word form chart on page 100.

1. stumble : walk :: _____ : speak

2. core : inside :: _____ : outside

3. noise : music :: _____ : words

4. take off : clothing :: _____ : words

5. strong : emotion :: _____ : speech

6. bright : color :: _____ : story

7. sharp : knife :: _____ : comment

E. In the blanks, write the most appropriate words from the word form chart on page 100.

    1. The medicine that the eye doctor put in my eyes made my vision

        _____ .

    2. Her ideas about the economy are _____ ; everyone laughs at them.

    3. My editor insists that I _____ all of the negative references to the government in my article; she wants only positive comments.

    4. He _____ copied the ten pages of text, letter by letter.

    5. That paper's articles are so _____ that I never trust that their content is true; they will write anything to attract more readers.

    6. Many people dislike his _____ remarks; they feel that his tongue is too sharp.

    7. The fire alarm was a(n) _____ ; there was no fire.

    8. Interviewers on the news should ask _____ questions in order to get a lot of information quickly.

    9. The ads for that movie were so _____ that my mother will not let me see it.

    10. I ran into two of my friends downtown, but I took their

        _____ and left them alone to talk.

F. Answer the following questions.

    1. Have you ever had a problem with stuttering? If so, what helped you?
    2. Describe a famous hoax that fooled many people.
    3. Have you ever had blurry vision? If so, why?
    4. Do you think that the news in this country is distorted? In your country?
    5. Name a topic which you feel vehemently about.
    6. Name someone who you think has a public facade quite different from his or her private life.
    7. Name something in the recent news that you think is absurd.
    8. Name a public figure who you think speaks caustically.
    9. Explain about some work or project which you have done that you found to be painstaking.
    10. Have you ever hinted to someone? Explain.
    11. Name a recent movie that you think was lurid.

WORDS FOR RECOGNITION

KEY WORD	SYNONYMS
confused (adj)	garbled
dig (v)	delve
doubting (adj)	skeptical
find out (v)	ascertain, glean
from now on (adv)	henceforth
hint (n) (negative)	innuendo, insinuation
lurid (adj)	gruesome
think (v)	reckon (colloq.)
relevant (adj)	germane, pertinent
say (v)	utter
see (v)	glimpse
show (v)	depict
spread (v)	disperse, dissecminate
start (v)	trigger
stutter (v)	stammer

Example Sentences

confused

The story was so garbled that I could not understand it.

dig

Reporters should delve deeply into the background of the stories that they are working on.

doubting

We were skeptical about the accuracy of the article because the facts did not seem to fit together well.

find out

The reporter ascertained that there had actually been three witnesses to the robbery.
She gleaned more information from the personnel records of the company.

from now on

Henceforth, the paper will be ready for sale by six o'clock each morning.

hint (negative)

> The innuendo in his testimony implied that his boss had instructed him to destroy the records.
>
> I became very angry at her insinuation that I had done something wrong.

lurid

> The account of the murder was quite gruesome; after reading it, I did not want to be alone in the house.

relevant

> That paragraph is not germane to the rest of the article.
>
> Be sure to include all of the pertinent information in your description of the scene of the crime.

say

> Every word that he uttered was false.

see

> The witnesses only glimpsed the murderer briefly.

show

> That movie depicts life two centuries ago.

spread

> The news is dispersed through a variety of channels.
>
> This information should be rapidly disseminated.

start

> The announcement triggered a panic.

stutter

> She stammers when she speaks.

think

> The gas station attendant reckoned that the highway was four miles up the road.

Exercises

G. Circle the word that is least related in meaning.

1. lurid   gruesome   skeptical
2. garbled   germane   pertinent
3. ascertain   glean   reckon
4. delve   disperse   disseminate
5. stammer   start   trigger
6. show   depict   glimpse
7. innuendo   henceforth   insinuation
8. skeptical   garbled   doubting

H. Write the key word for each set of words.

1. pertinent   germane   _____
2. disperse   disseminate   _____
3. insinuation   innuendo   _____
4. ascertain   glean   _____

I. Write the key word that corresponds to each italicized word.

1. Their questions *delved* into many areas. _____
2. It was a *gruesome* scene. _____
3. *Henceforth*, the editorials will occupy two full pages. _____
4. What *triggered* the problem? _____
5. She *stammered* an answer. _____
6. The basic facts should be *disseminated*. _____
7. Her *insinuations* are not true. _____
8. What can we *glean* from this photo? _____
9. Do you *reckon* that they will return? _____
10. He *uttered* only one word. _____
11. This article is *garbled*. _____
12. I am *skeptical* of his honesty. _____

J.   Write **T** if the sentence is true and **F** if it is false.

—— **1.** A gruesome movie may frighten children.

—— **2.** You should be skeptical of something that is obviously true.

—— **3.** A garbled speech is easy to understand.

—— **4.** Detectives glean evidence from witnesses to crimes.

—— **5.** A good news article should contain all the pertinent facts.

—— **6.** The purpose of the media is to disseminate information.

—— **7.** People are usually happy to hear insinuations about themselves.

—— **8.** The illustrations in magazines often depict important aspects of the article.

—— **9.** A news article can trigger a public reaction.

—— **10.** Students should not delve into their books.

K.   Answer the following questions.

1. Are gruesome movies popular in your country? Why or why not?
2. When do you become skeptical of what politicians say?
3. What does your favorite movie depict?
4. What topic would you like to delve into?
5. Do newspapers in your country print insinuations that are not yet proven? What is your opinion of this practice?
6. Who do you reckon is the most famous living person in your country?
7. How is most news disseminated in your country?
8. In the history of your country, what has triggered major changes?
9. How do you think that you can ascertain whether the news that you are reading or seeing is accurate?

Review Exercise

L. Read the passage and fill in the blanks with the appropriate words from the word form chart on page 100. Then, answer the questions that follow.

The coming of the age of television has brought major changes in the news that Americans get each day. In the past, news was disseminated primarily through the printed media, that is, the daily newspaper. However, today's research shows that a large percentage of Americans receive most of their news through television. Critics of television news argue that the newspaper format permits reporters to (1) _____ much more deeply into their subject and results in a much more (2) _____ report. They charge that because of television's constant worries about attracting large audiences, the television news is (3) _____ , with the news stories that are (4) _____ occupying most of the broadcasts. They suggest that the more boring background information on big stories is often (5) _____ in order to leave more time for (6) _____ films of crime scenes which will entertain the public. However, television investigative reporters respond that their research is just as (7) _____ as that of newspaper reporters. They argue that television can depict a news event more completely than newspapers can and insist that their reports contain all of the information that is germane to each story. In any case, while many may be skeptical of the quality of television news, undoubtedly Americans will continue to use it as their major news source.

1. How was news spread in the past? _____

_____

2. Why do critics feel that television news is distorted? _____

_____

3. What do television reporters say about their research? _____

_____

4. What do television reporters feel is the advantage of television news? _____

_____

Food

WORDS FOR PRODUCTION

Word Form Chart

NOUN	VERB	ADJECTIVE	ADVERB
abstention	abstain		
craving	crave		
fast	fast	fasting	
	gorge		
	grind	ground	
hoard	hoard	hoarded	
intoxication	intoxicate	intoxicated	
		intoxicating	intoxicatingly
ration	ration	rationed	
sauce			
shred	shred	shredded	
sobriety		sober	soberly
	spoil	spoiled	
staleness		stale	
staple			

Definitions and Examples

1. **abstain** [to deliberately not take some action]

   Abstention from drinking alcohol is a part of some religions.
   Vegetarians abstain from eating meat.

2. **crave** [to greatly want]

     I gained weight because of my craving for sweets.

     People who are alcoholics may crave alcohol but should not drink it.

3. **fast** [to abstain from food]

     Her fast has lasted for several days so far; she is trying to lose weight, but I am afraid that she will make herself sick.

     Some of the prisoners are fasting to protest the poor conditions in the prison.

     The fasting prisoners have become quite weak after ten days without food.

4. **gorge** [to eat greedily]

     It is unpleasant to watch him eat because he always gorges himself.

5. **grind** [to reduce to a powder or small pieces by friction]

     The mother had to grind up the tablet and hide it in the child's food because the little girl refused to take the pill.

     That restaurant serves only freshly ground coffee.

6. **hoard** [to hide a supply or fund]

     Their hoard of food would last them for a month in an emergency.

     The government asked the people not to hoard food in spite of the shortages caused by the war.

     A thief discovered the hoarded money and took it.

7. **intoxicated** [excited or dulled by alcohol or drugs; drunk]

     His state of intoxication was caused by beer.

     It is bad to drive when you are intoxicated.

     The intoxicated man could not stand up without support.

     This drug has a strong intoxicating effect.

8. **ration** [a food allowance determined by a limited supply]

     During the war, our family's sugar ration was one pound per month.

     The government is planning to ration gasoline if the supply gets any shorter.

     Each family is issued tickets each month to purchase the rationed goods.

9. **sauce** [a liquid topping for food]

     My favorite dessert is ice cream with chocolate sauce.

10. **shred** [to break or tear into long, narrow pieces]

     There were shreds of chicken in the soup.

     The recipe said to shred the lettuce.

     The shredded documents were carefully burned.

11. **sober** [not intoxicated]

> The police stopped the speeding driver and gave him a sobriety test.
> After drinking that much beer, he will not be sober until morning.

12. **spoil** [to go bad; to decay]

> We left the chicken salad sandwiches in the hot car and they spoiled.
> If you eat that spoiled food, you will get sick.

13. **stale** [tasteless or not fresh]

> The staleness of the cookies was obvious: they had no taste.
> The bread went stale two days after we bought it.

14. **staple** [one of the principal foods eaten by a group of people]

> The government tries to keep the prices of bread and meat low because
> they are the staples of the people's diets there.

Exercises

A. Write **T** if the sentence is true and **F** if it is false.

_____ **1.** Rice is a staple in many Asian countries.

_____ **2.** We refrigerate food to keep it from spoiling.

_____ **3.** People who often gorge themselves will probably be underweight.

_____ **4.** Drinking alcohol will make you sober.

_____ **5.** When you crave something, you do not like it.

_____ **6.** People who are fasting abstain from food.

_____ **7.** Drinking alcohol makes people intoxicated.

_____ **8.** Fresh bread is usually stale.

_____ **9.** A sauce is eaten with other foods.

_____ **10.** Governments usually encourage people to hoard food.

B. Answer each question with a word from the word form chart on page 110.

1. What do you have if you feel that you must eat a particular food?
2. What is your condition if you have drunk a lot of wine?
3. What may people do if they fear a shortage of food?
4. What is the condition of old bread?
5. What can you put on a plain piece of meat?
6. How do butchers make hamburger from a piece of beef?
7. What are you doing if you do not eat anything? (two answers)
8. What is a small, long piece of meat?
9. What may a government do to control the sale of a food that is in short supply?
10. What kind of foods do people depend on most?
11. What is a person doing that is eating too much?

C. Circle the word that is least related in meaning.

1. abstention   portion   ration

2. tear   spoil   shred

3. crave   desire   grind

4. staple   stale   old

5. drunk   intoxicated   fasting

6. hoard   keep   abstain

7. eat   spoil   gorge

D. Complete each analogy with a word from the word form chart on page 110.

1. meat : rotten :: bread : _____

2. like : love :: want : _____

3. love : hate :: drunk : _____

4. required : course :: _____ : food

5. budget : money :: _____ : food

6. rest : exercise :: _____ : food

7. infect : sick :: _____ : drunk

E. In the blanks, write the most appropriate words from the word form chart on page 110.

1. The government decided to _____ staple foods during the war so that their distribution would be fair.

2. Public _____ is against the law in some countries, so people in those places do not drink in the street.

3. Many children _____ candy.

4. If you _____ yourself, you may become ill.

5. The woman gave the _____ bread to the birds.

6. The man had a secret _____ of food that he refused to share with his neighbors after the disaster.

7. There were only small _____ of meat in the soup.

8. The _____ which was served on the meat was quite sweet.

9. Nowadays, few people _____ their own meat; they buy it in stores, ready to use.

10. Some people _____ for religious reasons, while others do it to lose weight.

F. Answer the following questions.

1. Has there been any rationing in your country recently? Explain.
2. Does your religion require you to abstain from any particular food or drink? Explain.
3. What are the staple foods in your country?
4. Have you ever fasted? Explain.
5. Is sobriety heavily valued in your culture? What is the attitude toward intoxicated people? (For example, is public intoxication illegal?)
6. Do you ever have cravings for particular foods? Explain.
7. Are foods in your country often eaten with sauces? Explain.

WORDS FOR RECOGNITION

KEY WORD	SYNONYMS
bar (n)	saloon, tavern
chew (v)	gnaw, munch
chop (v)	dice, mince
contaminated (adj)	tainted
drink (alcohol) (v)	imbibe
eat (hungrily) (v)	devour
feast (n)	banquet
(very) hungry (adj)	ravenous
mix (v & n)	blend

Example Sentences

bar

They spent the evening drinking beer in a local saloon.
This tavern serves simple food as well as drinks.

chew

The child was happily gnawing on a chocolate bar.
I like to munch on raw vegetables while I am cooking dinner.

chop

The recipe said to dice the meat and add it to the soup.
This salad has minced onions on top.

contaminated

That meat smells tainted; do not eat it.

drink

He imbibes more alcohol than is good for him.

devour

The starving people quickly devoured the meal.

feast

A large variety of foods was served at the banquet.

hungry

They were ravenous after their long hike.

mix

The chef blended the ingredients for the cake.

Exercises

G. Circle the word that is least related in meaning.

1. imbibe   eat   devour
2. tainted   ravenous   contaminated
3. tavern   bar   banquet
4. blend   gnaw   chew
5. chop   mince   munch
6. drink   devour   imbibe
7. tainted   hungry   ravenous
8. mix   dice   blend

H. Write the key word for each set of words.

1. munch   gnaw   _____
2. saloon   tavern   _____
3. mince   dice   _____

I. Write the key word that corresponds to each italicized word.

1. By the time dinner began, I was *ravenous*. _____
2. The *tainted* food went to waste. _____
3. The *saloon* was full of people. _____
4. The *banquet* lasted for three hours. _____
5. The lion *gnawed* on the bone. _____
6. The meat should be *minced*. _____
7. *Blend* the two liquids. _____
8. She *imbibes* regularly. _____
9. They *devoured* the steaks. _____
10. The children want something to *munch* on until dinner.

_____

J.   Write **T** if the sentence is true and **F** if it is false.

_____ **1.** You should not eat tainted food.

_____ **2.** Imbibing alcohol will make you intoxicated.

_____ **3.** When you are ravenous, you do not want to devour food.

_____ **4.** You dice food with your teeth.

_____ **5.** People usually eat banquets in saloons.

_____ **6.** People imbibe in taverns.

_____ **7.** People often gnaw on soup.

_____ **8.** When a recipe says to blend two ingredients, you should mix them together.

_____ **9.** You use a knife to munch food.

K.   Answer the following questions.

1. When do you usually feel ravenous?

2. Are there any taverns or saloons near here? Do they also serve food? Describe them.

3. What do you like to munch on while watching television?

4. How can you keep food from becoming tainted?

5. For what types of occasions do people in your country hold banquets?

6. What types of drinks do you regularly imbibe?

Review Exercise

L. Read the passage and fill in the words from the chart on page 110. Then answer the questions that follow.

The Volstead Act of the 1920s was the beginning of a great social experiment in the United States, but an experiment that failed miserably. This act of Congress made it illegal to sell or imbibe alcohol in the United States and was supported by many people who themselves (1) _____ from alcohol. These people felt that a(n) (2) _____ America would be a better America and thus wished to outlaw alcohol and the (3) _____ caused by it. However, those people who had had the custom of drinking (4) _____ alcohol and continued to get it wherever they could. With the nation's saloons and taverns closed, people bought alcohol from the criminals who were illegally making and importing it. Because the illegal production of alcohol was not being regulated, such alcohol was often of inferior quality and even tainted, resulting in sickness or death for many people. Eventually the government realized that the experiment in national abstinence was not working, and alcohol once again was legalized.

1. What was outlawed by the Volstead Act? _____

_____

2. Who was in favor of the new law? _____

_____

3. What were forced to close when the Volstead Act was in force? _____

_____

4. What were the problems with the illegal alcohol? _____

_____

Crime (B)

WORDS FOR PRODUCTION

Word Form Chart

NOUN	VERB	ADJECTIVE	ADVERB
blackmail	blackmail	blackmailed	
blackmailer			
evader	evade	evaded	
evasion		evasive	evasively
	incriminate	incriminating	
		incriminated	incriminatingly
intimidation	intimidate	intimidating	
		intimidated	
malice		malicious	maliciously
molestation	molest	molested	
molester			
notoriety		notorious	notoriously
notoriousness			
ordeal			
rape	rape	raped	
rapist			
riot	riot	riotous	riotously
rioter			
strangulation	strangle	strangled	
strangler			
	thwart	thwarted	

Definitions and Examples

1. **blackmail** [to force someone to pay money in exchange for not revealing negative information about that person]

    There are laws against blackmail in the United States, but many victims are too frightened to go to the police.
    The blackmailer demanded $10,000 for his silence.
    She was blackmailed for ten years by someone who had witnessed her crime.
    The blackmailed man finally refused to pay any more, and admitted his secret to his wife.

2. **evade** [to escape or avoid doing something that should be done]

    Many people try to evade paying their taxes.
    Tax evasion is a common crime.
    During the Vietnam War, many U.S. draft evaders went to Canada to live.
    Evaded taxes cost the government a lot of money.

3. **incriminate** [to show involvement in a crime]

    In the United States, an arrested suspect must be warned that anything he says may be used to incriminate him.
    The evidence found at the scene of the crime was quite incriminating, so the police arrested her.
    The incriminated woman demanded to see a lawyer.

4. **intimidate** [to frighten by making threats]

    The robber's attempt to intimidate his victim failed and she screamed for help and ran away.
    The criminal's intimidation of the witnesses frightened them so much that they refused to testify against him in court.

5. **malice** (a) [a desire to see another suffer]

    The kidnapper maliciously refused to let the parents talk to their child on the phone.

    (b) [intent to commit an unlawful act]

    Although he had killed the child, the judge decided that there had been no malice, and the child's death had been an unfortunate accident.
    The teenage boys admitted that their intent had been malicious when they had entered the old woman's house.

6. **molest** (a) [to annoy, disturb, or hurt, especially with hostile intent]

> The gangs of youths in the street were molesting the people who were trying to get to their cars; several people were robbed and several others were beaten.

(b) [to make unwanted sexual advances to; to force sex on]

> The woman was beaten and sexually molested.
> Many cases of child molestation are reported each year.
> The child molester should be imprisoned and given psychiatric treatment.
> The molested woman gave a description of her attacker to the police.

7. **notorious** [widely and unfavorably known]

> He was notorious for his many crimes.
> Criminals should avoid notoriety if they do not want to get caught.
> The bank robber is notoriously clever.
> The notoriousness of his crimes is still spreading.

8. **ordeal** [a painful experience]

> They did not press charges because they wanted to avoid the ordeal of a trial.

9. **rape** [to force the act of sex on a person]

> She was raped by a man with a knife, who told her that he would kill her if she struggled.
> The rapist was sentenced to ten years in prison.
> Many rapes are not reported to the police because the victim does not want to relive the ordeal in court.
> The raped woman was afraid to stay alone in her apartment at night.

10. **riot** [a violent public disorder]

> There was a riot after the crowded rock concert and several people were hurt.
> The prisoners rioted during their exercise hour and two convicts escaped.
> The rioters broke store windows and stole some of the goods inside.

11. **riotous** [unrestrained]

> The teenagers' behavior at the party was riotous and some of the furniture was damaged.
> The audience laughed riotously at the jokes.

12. **strangle** [to kill or die by interference with breathing]

> The murderer strangled his victim with his bare hands.
> The victim died by strangulation.
> The police are searching for the murderer whom the press have named "The Strangler."
> The strangled man lay on the floor of his bedroom.

13. **thwart** [to effectively oppose or confuse]

> The thieves' scheme to rob the bank was thwarted by the police.

Exercises

A. Write **T** if the sentence is true and **F** if it is false.

_____ 1. A notorious person is famous for bad actions.

_____ 2. Strangulation is one method of murder.

_____ 3. People evade receiving money for their work.

_____ 4. Blackmailers intimidate their victims.

_____ 5. Torture is one type of ordeal.

_____ 6. People may be injured during a riot.

_____ 7. A person is happy when his plans are thwarted.

_____ 8. Rape is a violent crime.

_____ 9. A molested person is a criminal.

_____ 10. People wish to be incriminated.

B. Answer each question with a word from the word form chart on page 119.

1. What do the police try to do to criminals' plans?
2. What may occur if a large crowd is uncontrolled?
3. Who might use a rope to murder someone?
4. What do criminals often feel toward their victims?
5. What do criminals try to do to the law?
6. What are threats an example of?
7. Which crimes are examples of sexual violence?
8. Which crime does not usually involve violence?
9. What does evidence do to a guilty person?

C. Circle the word that is least related in meaning.

1. assault   malice   rape
2. steal   molest   embezzle
3. evil   malice   torture
4. avoid   rape   evade
5. ordeal   intimidation   threat
6. thwart   stop   riot
7. molest   hurt   blackmail
8. incriminating   notorious   famous

D. In the blanks, write the most appropriate words from the word form chart on page 119.

1. The trip through the desert without water was a three-day

   _____ .

2. The kidnapper felt so much _____ toward his victim that he tortured and killed him.

3. His attempt at embezzlement was _____ by his secretary, who noticed his incorrect entries in the records.

4. The assassin _____ capture for two weeks, but was eventually caught.

5. The _____ of the prisoner lasted for five hours. By then the police had all the information that they needed to arrest the rest of the gang.

6. The woman paid one thousand dollars per month to her

   _____ for two years before she found the courage to go to the police.

7. That gang has so _____ the people in this neighborhood that they rarely leave their homes after dark.

8. That man has so much _____ that he is recognized everywhere as a criminal.

9. Several buildings were set on fire during the _____ .

10. The testimony of several witnesses _____ her.

E. Answer the following questions.

1. What is the worst ordeal that you have ever experienced?
2. Name a notorious person in the history of your country.
3. Have there been any riots in your country recently? If so, what caused them?
4. What is the worst crime problem in your city? What do the police do to thwart the crimes?
5. Are many rapes reported to the police in your country? Why or why not?
6. Which laws in your country are frequently evaded? Why?
7. In your country, for what reasons are people often blackmailed?

WORDS FOR RECOGNITION

KEY WORD	SYNONYMS
anger (n)	fury, indignation, ire, wrath
annoy (v)	harass, irk, vex
argue (v)	dispute, quarrel, squabble
arrest (v)	apprehend
awful (adj)	abominable, appalling, atrocious, dreadful
beat (v)	batter, pummel
blackmail (n)	extortion
charge (v) (with a crime)	arraign, indict
escape (v)	flee
malice (n)	spite, grudge, malevolence
theft (n)	larceny

Example Sentences

anger

We could see the fury on his face when he saw his damaged car.
His indignation at my stupid remark was evident from his tone of voice.
Her ire grew even worse when I continued to argue with her.
Her wrath was so great that she could barely speak.

annoy

I have been harassed by nuisance telephone calls recently.
His negative attitude irked us.
The teacher was vexed by his students' lack of concern about their studies.

argue

That group is disputing the company's right to dump waste in the river.
The men were quarreling about who had won the game.
The children were squabbling over the new toy.

arrest

The police apprehended the suspect just ten minutes after the robbery
   occurred.

awful

>   Everyone agrees that the assassin's crime was abominable.
>   The story of their ordeal during the kidnapping was appalling.
>   The atrocious behavior of the rapist was condemned by his family.
>   We read in the paper about the dreadful strangulation murders.

beat

>   The victim was battered by his attacker.
>   The secret police pummeled the man during their interrogation of him.

blackmail

>   That criminal has been convicted of extortion; he forced people to pay him
>   money in exchange for keeping their activities secret.

charge

>   The bank president has been arraigned on charges of embezzlement.
>   The men that the police arrested will be indicted on a variety of charges
>   tomorrow.

escape

>   The prisoners tried to flee on foot from the prison.

malice

>   He stole the money from his employer out of spite.
>   Because she has a grudge against that family, she tried to kidnap their baby.
>   His malevolence caused him to try to hurt everyone that he came into contact
>   with.

theft

>   He was arrested for larceny when they caught him with the stolen paintings.

Exercises

F.   Circle the word that is least related in meaning.

1. arraign   squabble   quarrel   dispute
2. dreadful   irked   abominable   atrocious
3. pummel   indict   batter
4. ire   fury   wrath   assailant
5. skulk   malevolence   spite   grudge
6. irk   dispute   vex   harass
7. larceny   dispute   theft

G.   Write the key word for each set of words.

1. arraign   indict   _____

2. batter   pummel   _____

3. ire   wrath   _____

4. quarrel   squabble   _____

5. irk   vex   _____

6. appalling   atrocious   _____

7. grudge   spite   _____

8. abominable   dreadful   _____

9. indignation   fury   _____

H.   Write the key word which corresponds to each italicized word.

1. Her *wrath* grew as she heard the whole story. _____

2. He was *irked* by the lawyer's questions. _____

3. His *extortion* victim went to the police. _____

4. She was *indicted* for murder. _____

5. It was an *abominable* crime. _____

6. The *battered* woman called the police. _____

7. She was arrested and charged with *larceny*. _____

8. The thieves attempted to *flee*. _____

9. Their *dispute* has lasted for years. _____

I.   Write **T** if the sentence is true and **F** if it is false.

_____   **1.** People are often intimidated by threats.

_____   **2.** People sometimes yell because they are indignant.

_____   **3.** A person is arraigned before he is apprehended.

_____   **4.** If his victim yells, an assailant may flee.

_____   **5.** Pummeling a person will not hurt that person.

_____   **6.** A clever criminal will vex the police.

_____   **7.** Wrath can lead to quarrels.

_____   **8.** An abominable crime will not cause ire in the community.

_____   **9.** A successful extortionist gets money from his victim.

_____   **10.** Larceny is a more serious crime than stealing.

J. Answer the following questions.

1. What frequently irks you?
2. What recent event did you think was appalling?
3. Whom do you often quarrel with?
4. What do you do to calm down if you are really furious at someone?
5. Is wife-battering a problem in your country? Explain.
6. Have you ever had a grudge against anyone? Explain.
7. What do you think is the best way to end a squabble with a friend?
8. What is a typical punishment for larceny in your country?
9. What percentage of criminals are apprehended in your country? Do you think that the police are efficient?

Review Exercise for Units 1 and 14

K. In the blanks, write the most appropriate words from the word form charts on pages 3 and 119. Then answer the questions following the passage.

At approximately two o'clock this morning, two notorious criminals escaped from the state penitentiary. Police identified one of the escaped felons as Harold Winger, who was convicted two years ago of (1) _____ six women to death with a piece of wire. The other escapee has been identified as William Harris, a former bank employee convicted six months ago of (2) _____ $300,000 from the bank where he worked. The escape occurred during a (3) _____ that started at the prison after the convicts had been released from their cells and taken to the prison yard because of a fire, apparently started by one of the inmates. Winger and Harris (4) _____ a guard, took his gun, and forced their way out of the main gate.

Roadblocks were set up around the prison to try to apprehend the two fleeing men, but so far the two have (5) _____ all the traps set for them. Officials at the prison are now (6) _____ the cellmates of Winger and Harris to find out what their escape plans were.

Police are somewhat surprised that Harris, whose crime was nonviolent and who had been a cooperative prisoner, chose to team up with Winger for his escape. Police describe Winger as an extremely violent man who talked often of taking (7) _____ against those who had sent him to jail. In fact, even at his trial, Winger had shouted his intentions of retribution as the judge was reading his sentence. In short, police consider Winger to be a menace to all law-abiding citizens, and hope that he will soon be apprehended.

1. Who do police think started the fire at the penitentiary? _____
   _____

2. What was the purpose of the roadblocks? Were they successful? _____
   _____

3. How are the prison officials trying to find out about the escape? _____
   _____

4. What threat has Winger made? _____
   _____

Work (B)

WORDS FOR PRODUCTION

Word Form Chart

NOUN	VERB	ADJECTIVE	ADVERB
delegation	delegate	delegated	
foreboding	forbode		
havoc			
hazard		hazardous	hazardously
incentive			
ingenuity		ingenious	ingeniously
meagerness		meager	meagerly
		menial	menially
pettiness		petty	
picket	picket	picketing	
strenuousness		strenuous	strenuously

Definitions and Examples

1. **delegate** [to assign responsibility or authority to another]

    The proper delegation of duties will be discussed at the first project meeting.
    A good boss must be willing to delegate many tasks.

2. **foreboding** [a negative prediction or feeling concerning the future]

    I hope that my foreboding about the future of the company is wrong.
    The recent drop in sales forbodes a bad year for us.

3. **havoc** [wide and general confusion or destruction]

   The strike has played havoc with our delivery schedule; nothing is being delivered on time.

   The storm wreaked havoc in the town, destroying trees and blowing out windows.

4. **hazard** (a) [a source of danger]

   The faster pace of the assembly line is a hazard to the workers.
   Some employees earn higher wages if their jobs are hazardous.
   He operated the machine hazardously and injured one of his co-workers.

   (b) [to risk (a guess)]

   We cannot yet hazard a guess about when the product will be ready to be introduced to the market.

5. **incentive** [something that pushes a person to work]

   The basic incentive for most workers is their paycheck.

6. **ingenious** [marked by a special aptitude at discovering or inventing]

   Being an inventor requires a lot of ingenuity.
   Everyone agreed that her plan was an ingenious one and would work.
   They ingeniously outlined a plan by which both the union and the management would benefit.

7. **meager** [deficient in quality or quantity]

   The union is disturbed by the meagerness of new ideas being put forth by the management.
   Her meager salary will not support her family.
   Because they pay their workers so meagerly, no one wants to work for them.

8. **menial** [lowly; appropriate to a servant]

   She could find only menial, low-paying work when she came to this country.

9. **petty** [having little or no importance]

   My boss gets very upset over petty problems.
   The pettiness of his complaints surprised us.

10. **picket** [a person posted by a union at a place of work affected by a strike]

    The many pickets outside the factory prevented the nonunion workers from entering.
    They are picketing the company in their attempt to get higher wages.
    The picketing workers yelled insults at those who tried to cross the picket line.

11. **strenuous** [requiring strong physical effort]

The strenuousness of his new job quickly tired him out.
Regular, strenuous exercise is good for one's heart.
They strenuously objected to our proposal, and refused to even discuss it.

Exercises

A. Write **T** if the sentence is true and **F** if it is false.

_____ 1. Inventors must be ingenious.

_____ 2. Workers want meager wages.

_____ 3. Most errands are hazardous.

_____ 4. Mocking a person mollifies that person.

_____ 5. A petty reason is a good reason.

_____ 6. Bosses thank workers for creating havoc.

_____ 7. Menial jobs are often low-paying.

_____ 8. Most people do not enjoy crossing picket lines.

_____ 9. Money is a common incentive to work.

_____ 10. When you delegate a responsibility, you must take care of it yourself.

B. Answer each question with a word from the word form chart on page 129.

1. What makes you work hard?
2. What should you do with a responsibility that an underling can handle?
3. What do you need in order to think of clever solutions to problems?
4. What is something that you should be very careful of?
5. What is the opposite of "much"?
6. What kind of complaint may not be acted on?
7. What do you call a person stationed outside a factory to demonstrate protest?
8. What kind of job requires a lot of strength?
9. What may you have concerning the future?

C. Circle the word that is least related to the others in meaning.

1. menial   dangerous   hazardous

2. mess   incentive   havoc

3. small   petty   tardy

4. mollify   delegate   calm

5. heavy   meager   strenuous

6. hazardous   inventive   ingenious
7. incentive   purpose   pettiness
8. meager   small   menial

D. In the blanks, write the most appropriate words from the word form chart on page 129.

1. They are not satisfied with the _____ pay increase that they have been offered.

2. Working in that mine is too _____ ; so far this year, two men have been killed on the job.

3. He had many complaints, but they were all quite _____ . I doubt if we will take action on any of them.

4. The union members are _____ the factory because they are out on strike.

5. Her plan to save the business was _____ ; everyone was amazed at her cleverness.

6. The work is quite _____ ; the person that we hire will have to be strong.

7. That job is too important to _____ to an underling; the boss should take care of it himself.

8. The boss was not _____ by our excuses and continued to yell at us.

9. Her _____ for taking that job could not have been the salary; it is very low.

10. Her sense of _____ was proven wrong: the company was a success.

F. Answer the following questions.

1. Name some jobs that are hazardous and explain why.
2. Give an example of a petty complaint about a job.
3. If your boss is angry with you, what do you think is a good way to mollify him or her?
4. Give some examples of jobs that are considered to be menial in your country.
5. What are your incentives in your career?
6. Do people on strike picket in your country? Are there any laws concerning picketing? Do people cross the picket lines?
7. Describe the most strenuous task you have ever done.
8. Do you pay any attention to it if you have a feeling of foreboding?

WORDS FOR RECOGNITION

KEY WORD	SYNONYMS
brief (adj)	succinct, terse
complaint (n)	grievance, gripe, grumble
foreboding (n)	misgiving, premonition
hazardous (adj)	perilous, precarious
meager (adj)	scanty, skimpy, sparse
mollify (v)	appease, assuage, temper
muscular (adj)	brawny, burly
supervisor (n)	foreman
try (v)	endeavor, strive

Example Sentences

brief

The message from the union was succinct: no workers would report for work the next day.
The workers listened to the terse reply from the management.

complaint

The purpose of the meeting was to discuss our grievances.
Her worst gripe about her job is the low pay.
The boss listened carefully to the grumbles of his men.

foreboding

I have misgivings about this course of action.
His premonition that the company would fail came true.

hazardous

That course of action is a perilous one for the company; we may go out of business.
You should find a less precarious way to balance that machine.

meager

The benefits that they offer are quite scanty.
They cannot get good workers when they pay such skimpy wages.
Qualified people are sparse in this area.

muscular

We need someone who is brawny to move those boxes.
The burly men did not rest all morning.

supervisor

> The foreman showed me how to operate the machine safely.

try

> We are endeavoring to reopen the factory as soon as possible.
> You should strive to maintain proper safety procedures at all times.

Exercises

G.   Circle the word that is the least related to the others in meaning.

1. premonition   foreboding   misgiving   incentive
2. gripe   grievance   gain   grumble
3. skimpy   somber   sparse   scanty
4. terse   burly   succinct
5. gripe   endeavor   strive
6. precarious   perilous   petty
7. terse   burly   brawny

H.   Write the key word for each set of words.

1. succinct   terse   _____
2. brawny   burly   _____
3. endeavor   strive   _____
4. scanty   sparse   _____
5. precarious   perilous   _____
6. grumble   gripe   _____
7. misgiving   premonition   _____

I. Write the key word that corresponds to each italicized word.

1. The message was *terse*. _____

2. Their position is *precarious*. _____

3. She often has *premonitions*. _____

4. They are always *grumbling*. _____

5. There is *scant* pleasure in this job. _____

6. The *foreman* told me to work faster. _____

7. They have many *grievances*. _____

8. The portions were *skimpy*. _____

9. You must *strive* in order to achieve. _____

10. He is a *brawny* man. _____

J. Write **T** if the sentence is true and **F** if it is false.

_____ 1. Being brawny hinders a person's ability to do heavy labor.

_____ 2. People should strive for what they want in their lives.

_____ 3. People will pay scant attention to gripes which are petty.

_____ 4. Premonitions usually concern one's past.

_____ 5. Thin people are usually burly.

_____ 6. You should endeavor to do a perilous task carefully.

_____ 7. Clothing that is skimpy needs to be taken in.

_____ 8. A foreman supervises the work of others.

_____ 9. People do not like to listen to gripes.

_____ 10. People feel very positive when they have misgivings.

K. Answer the following questions.

1. Name someone who is brawny.
2. What grievances do you have about your family?
3. Have you ever had a premonition? Explain.
4. What do you strive to do in school?
5. Are you usually succinct when you speak?
6. Is the wearing of skimpy clothing by women considered acceptable in your country?
7. Describe the most perilous action you have ever taken.

Review Exercise for Units 2 and 15

L. In the blanks, write the most appropriate words from the word form charts on pages 12 and 129.

Yesterday, on his way out of the plant, John Smith received a terse message from his boss. John's foreman handed him the pink notice stating, "Do not report for work tomorrow. Pick up your final check today." John was not really surprised, as he had had a(n) (1) _____ all week that things were not working out well at his new job. John asked the foreman whether there was any chance that the boss might reconsider, but the foreman replied that the boss had been quite (2) _____ about his decision.

John realized that he had been foolish to take a job that he knew that he would not like. While in former job John had worked quite assiduously, his performance at this job was rather (4) _____ . He found himself (5) _____ over his coffee breaks and lunch hours and being (6) _____ at returning to work each time. As John is not a brawny man, he found the heavy work of his new job to be (7) _____ . Since he had not done this type of work before, he felt (8) _____ as he saw himself bungling one task after another. He felt even worse when his co-workers began to call him a(n) (9) _____ to their safety.

Now John is determined to find a better-paying and less (10) _____ job, one that has a future for him. He is sure that once he is involved again in work that he finds interesting, his recent poor work habits will disappear, and he will approach his tasks with the former assiduous attention to detail which he prided himself on.

War (B)

WORDS FOR PRODUCTION

Word Form Chart

NOUN	VERB	ADJECTIVE	ADVERB
belligerence		belligerent	belligerently
	cow	cowed	
debris			
detonation	detonate	detonated	
detonator			
infringement	infringe		
martyr	martyr	martyred	
obliteration	obliterate	obliterated	
onslaught			
partisan		partisan	
projectile			
quarters	quarter		
salute	salute	saluting	
subsidence	subside		
torpedo			

Definitions and Examples

1. **belligerence** [an aggressive or warlike attitude]

    The belligerence of that country's leaders may soon lead the country
      into war.
    Their belligerent attitude was evident from their frequent threats.
    They belligerently refused to withdraw the large military force that stood
      waiting at the border.

2. **cow** [to intimidate with threats or a show of force]

    The president was cowed by the army's show of force and agreed to give the military more power in the running of the country.
    The cowed defenders laid down their weapons and surrendered.

3. **debris** [the remains of something broken down or destroyed; ruins]

    Debris covered the street after the bombing.

4. **detonate** [to explode with sudden violence; to activate]

    The detonation of the bomb was done at a distance by radio control.
    The police detonated the unexploded bomb after taking it to a large, open field where no damage would occur.
    The detonated explosives leveled the building.
    The detonator of the bomb was broken, causing it to not explode.

5. **infringe** [to act in a way that violates the rights of others]

    The raid on the capital was an infringement of our national pride.
    Any infringement on the basic rights of the citizens by the new government will be strongly protested.

6. **martyr** [one who sacrifices his or her life for the sake of a cause]

    He is a martyr in the eyes of the nation because he died in the struggle against the invaders.
    Many people chose to be martyred rather than accept the rule of the conquerors.
    The martyred resistance fighters were buried at the site of their final battle.

7. **obliterate** [to destroy utterly so that nothing remains to be seen]

    Their intent was the obliteration of the native culture in the lands that they had conquered.
    The explosion obliterated the center of the town.
    The obliterated buildings will probably never be rebuilt.

8. **onslaught** [a very fierce attack]

    The onslaught of the enemy army began at dawn.

9. **partisan** [a strong supporter of a group, frequently a guerrilla operating within enemy territory]

    The partisans are based in the mountains outside of the town.

10. **projectile** [a body, pushed by an external force, that continues in motion, especially a body thrown by a weapon]

    The projectiles from this new type of gun can travel over two miles.

11. **quarter** [to provide with housing or shelter]

> The officers' quarters on this base are much nicer than those for the enlisted personnel.
> Many of the soldiers were quartered in private homes during the emergency.

12. **salute** [to position one's hand to show respect to a superior]

> The officer reprimanded the soldier because his salute was slow and not of the proper form.
> The privates saluted the approaching captain.

13. **subside** [to become quiet or less]

> The subsidence of the bombing was a welcome relief.
> The noise gradually subsided as we got farther from the battle.

14. **torpedo** [a marine projectile filled with an explosive]

> The torpedo blew a large hole in the side of the ship.

Exercises

A. Write **T** if the sentence is true and **F** if it is false.

_____ 1. An onslaught is a sign of respect for a superior officer.

_____ 2. Belligerence usually leads to a truce.

_____ 3. Debris is left after an explosion.

_____ 4. A salute shows respect.

_____ 5. A problem that is subsiding is getting worse.

_____ 6. People are cowed when they are afraid.

_____ 7. People get annoyed when someone infringes on their rights.

_____ 8. Torpedoes are generally used on land.

_____ 9. Martyrs are so loved by their countrymen that some people travel long distances to shake a martyr's hand.

_____ 10. A torpedo is a type of projectile.

_____ 11. Partisans do much of their fighting from hidden bases.

B.   Answer each question with a word from the word form chart on page 137.

     1. What do you use to set off an explosion?
     2. Who is a person who dies for his or her country?
     3. What is a weapon that ships carry?
     4. Who is a type of guerrilla?
     5. What may a bomb do to its target?
     6. What are bullets and torpedoes examples of?
     7. Where do soldiers sleep?
     8. What does a private greet an officer with?
     9. What kind of attitude leads to war?
     10. How may a conquered people feel?
     11. What kind of an attack is very strong?

C.   Circle the word that is least related in meaning.

     1. destroy   obliterate   martyr
     2. quarters   partisans   accommodations
     3. detonate   explode   cow
     4. subside   salute   greet
     5. projectile   debris   bullet
     6. infringement   attack   onslaught
     7. cow   frighten   salute

D.   Complete each analogy with a word from the word form chart on page 137.

     1. hurt : kill :: damage : _____
     2. television : turn on :: bomb : _____
     3. cold : pneumonia :: attack : _____
     4. current : past :: hero : _____
     5. cancer : disease :: torpedo : _____
     6. student : dormitory :: soldier : _____

E. In the blanks, write the most appropriate words from the word form chart on page 137.

1. The fighting should _____ soon because both sides are running out of ammunition.

2. The people in the town were totally _____ by the invaders and obeyed all of their commands without question.

3. She became a(n) _____ when she was struck down while defending the city.

4. That ship's most dangerous weapons are the _____ which it carries.

5. They consider our presence in their harbor as a(n) _____ on their shipping rights.

6. The _____ of the bomb was damaged and it did not go off.

7. There was so much _____ in the streets after the battle that they were almost impassable.

8. The government troops would like to capture the _____ who have been harrassing their bases with acts of sabotage.

F. Answer the following questions.

1. How do the soldiers in your country salute?
2. Name a martyr in the history of your country.
3. What would you do if you found a bomb which had not yet been detonated?
4. Name as many projectiles as you know the names for in English.
5. What would you consider to be an infringement of your personal rights?
6. How would you treat a teacher that had a belligerent attitude toward you?

WORDS FOR RECOGNITION

KEY WORD	SYNONYMS
belligerent (adj)	bellicose, combative, contentious
cautious (adj)	chary, wary
cow (v)	daunt
debris (n)	rubble
defeat (v)	rout, vanquish
die (v)	decease, perish
draft (v)	conscript
group (n)	squad
hate (v)	abhor, detest, loathe
infringe (v)	encroach, trespass
meet (v)	rendezvous
obey (v)	comply
subside (v)	abate, dwindle, taper

Example Sentences

belligerent

>Their bellicose attitude was evident from the quantity of weapons they carried.
>He has a very combative nature; he is always getting into fights.
>She is too contentious to be a good diplomat.

cautious

>They are chary of the promises of peace.
>The wary soldier kept his gun on his prisoner.

cow

>The people were not daunted by the invasion and took every opportunity to harrass the invaders.

debris

>Only a pile of rubble was left of the bombed building.

defeat

>They were quickly routed by the enemy's superior weapons.
>They vanquished all their opponents.

die

> The deceased were taken away to be buried.
> Many soldiers perished in the battle.

draft

> They conscripted many men into the army at the start of the war.

group

> The squad of soldiers marched onto the training field.

hate

> Most people abhor war.
> He detested army life.
> He loathes the idea of killing people.

infringe

> They attacked when we encroached on their border.
> We trespassed on their territory by accident.

meet

> We will rendezvous with the other squad on the west side of the town.

obey

> I must insist that you comply with my wishes.

subside

> The fighting abated as the sun set.
> The number of hourly casualties dwindled to almost nonc.
> Experts predict that the intensity of the fighting will taper off as winter
>   sets in.

Exercises

G. Circle the word that is least related in meaning.

1. daunt   perish   decease

2. encroach   comply   trespass

3. chary   conscript   wary

4. taper   loathe   abhor

5. vanquish   detest   rout

6. combative   bellicose   rubble

7. dwindle   detest   abate

H. Write the key word for each set of words.

1. loathe   detest   _____
2. rout   vanquish   _____
3. wary   chary   _____
4. decease   perish   _____
5. combative   contentious   _____
6. trespass   encroach   _____

I. Write the key word that corresponds to each italicized word.

1. The *squad* moved quickly out of sight. _____
2. The people appeared to be a bit *daunted* by what had happened.

   _____

3. They *complied* with her orders immediately. _____
4. The building was reduced to a pile of *rubble.* _____
5. Our *rendezvous* will be at midnight. _____
6. No one likes his *bellicose* manner. _____.
7. They plan to *conscript* another 2,000 men. _____
8. The new laws *encroached* on their area of responsibility.

   _____

9. Many people have *perished* in the fighting. _____
10. We are *wary* of their offer. _____
11. The problems should *abate* soon. _____
12. They were totally *routed.* _____

J. Write **T** if the sentence is true and **F** if it is false.

____ 1. People want to be vanquished.
____ 2. People do not want to do things that they detest.
____ 3. People are buried after they perish.
____ 4. Officers want their men to comply with their orders.
____ 5. An army conscripts men when it does not need any more soldiers.
____ 6. A country should be wary of a bellicose neighboring country.
____ 7. It is a good idea to encroach on another's territory.
____ 8. People want rubble on their street.
____ 9. One person can rendezvous.
____ 10. If your supplies dwindle, you need to get more supplies.

———— **11.** People may be daunted by an onslaught.

———— **12.** One man can be a squad.

K. Answer the following questions.

1. What do you find to be daunting?
2. Do you think that a soldier should always comply with his orders? If not, under what circumstances should he refuse to comply?
3. Does your country's military have conscripts or only volunteers?
4. Describe something that you are chary about.
5. Do you know any people who are contentious? How do you deal with them?
6. Describe a situation that you loathe.
7. How far does the law in your country permit an owner to go in protecting his property against trespassers?
8. Describe a problem in your country that has recently abated.

Review Exercise for Units 3 and 16

L. In the blanks, write the most appropriate words from the word form charts on pages 21 and 137.

During the 1980s, governments worldwide were faced with an increase in terrorist activity. Terrorist attacks, ranging from the ambush and murder of individual government officials to the (1) ———————— of bombs in government offices, prompted much discussion of how governments could effectively (2) ———————— against such acts. The decision on how to react to openly hostile actions is always a difficult one, even when the targets of possible reprisals are obvious, as in the case of an attack by a(n) (3) ———————— neighboring country, but it is especially hard when the attacker is an unknown individual or organization.

While most government leaders agree that terrorists must be punished if terrorism is to (4) ———————— , there is little agreement on how to carry out such punishment without (5) ———————— on the rights of many ordinary, peaceful (6) ———————— . A variety of preventative measures have been taken, such as the posting of more sentries at government buildings and military installations, and the formation of special military (7) ———————— , trained to respond to terrorist incidents once one has arisen. In any case, there is a growing awareness that in order not to be (8) ———————— by this onslaught of terrorism, both governments and their citizens must be increasingly wary of situations where the posibility of terrorism exists.

Family (B)

WORDS FOR PRODUCTION

Word Form Chart

NOUN	VERB	ADJECTIVE	ADVERB
adultery		adulterous	
clan		clannish	clannishly
courtship	court	courting	
emulation	emulate		
heirloom			
illegitimacy		illegitimate	
monogamy		monogamous	monogamously
polygamy		polygamous	polygamously
polygamist			
seduction	seduce		
spouse			
suitor			

Definitions and Examples

1. **adultery** [voluntary sexual activity between a married person and someone that he or she is not married to]

   She suspected her husband of committing adultery after she saw him having lunch with another woman.

   He divorced his wife because of her adulterous behavior.

2. **clan** [a group strongly united by a common interest or common characteristics; a family group]

> Our whole clan gets together to celebrate Christmas.
> That group is very clannish; they do not accept outsiders easily.
> When John married Mary, she felt that his family behaved very clannishly and did not make her feel welcome.

3. **court** [to seek the affections of]

> He has been courting her for over a year; I think that he will ask her to get married soon.

4. **emulate** [to imitate; to try to equal or excel]

> Emulation of a hero is common among teenagers.
> He emulates his father and tries to excel in the same sports that his father played in school.

5. **heirloom** [something of special value handed down from one generation to the next]

> This watch is a family heirloom: My grandfather received it on his first birthday and then gave it to my father when he was twenty-one.

6. **illegitimate** [born of parents who are not married; illegal]

> The boy was ashamed of his illegitimacy and told everyone that his father had died when he was a baby.
> Illegitimate children in some countries do not have many legal rights.

7. **monogamy** [the state or custom of being married to one person at a time]

> Societies that practice monogamy have smaller families than those which do not.
> When he divorced his wife, he told her that he did not wish to remain monogamous.
> The law in the United States specifies that people must live monogamously.

8. **polygamy** [the state or custom of being married to more than one person at a time]

> Islam permits the practice of polygamy.
> Polygamous marriages often produce many children.
> After polygamy was outlawed in the United States, many people who were living polygamously moved to other countries.
> He was accused of being a polygamist and arrested.

9. **seduce** [to persuade to disloyalty or disobedience; to persuade to engage in sexual activity]

> The father was intent on preventing the seduction of his daughter by the handsome young man.
> He was seduced by the quantity of money he was offered to betray his country.

10. **spouse** [a husband or a wife]

> The professors' spouses were also invited to the picnic.

11. **suitor** [one who courts a woman or seeks to marry her]

> She has had many suitors over the past few years, but she has not married any of them.

Exercises

A. Write **T** if the sentence is true and **F** if it is false.

_____ 1. A suitor courts a woman when he wants to marry her.

_____ 2. A polygamist has more than one spouse.

_____ 3. A clan is a group of small children.

_____ 4. When you hate someone, you usually try to emulate that person.

_____ 5. People often treasure family heirlooms.

_____ 6. Any child born in a monogamous marriage is illegitimate.

_____ 7. Most wives want their husbands to be adulterous.

_____ 8. Parents usually want their daughters to be seduced.

_____ 9. A person is married to his or her spouse.

B. Answer each question with a word from the word form chart on page 146.

1. What kind of marriage is between only two people?
2. What is a husband or a wife?
3. What is often considered to be grounds for divorce?
4. What kind of child may not receive an inheritance?
5. What can you call a group of related people?
6. What may a mother give to her daughter?
7. What kind of marriage involves at least three people?
8. Who courts a woman?
9. What kind of behavior is imitative?

C. Circle the word that is least related in meaning.

1. seduce   emulate   persuade

2. illustrative   illegal   illegitimate

3. husband   suitor   spouse

4. gift   seduction   heirloom

5. court   imitate   emulate

6. clan   group   suitor

7. unfaithful   adulterous   monogamous

D. In the blanks, write the most appropriate words from the word form chart on page 146.

1. Her husband's affair with his secretary was a clear case of

   _____ .

2. You should try to _____ the behavior of successful people in your field.

3. Her current _____ wants her to marry him, but she has not yet decided whether she will.

4. She was _____ by her charming boyfriend and later regretted running away to New York with him.

5. My family is such a big _____ that we can hardly fit in the house when we all return home for holidays.

6. He sees the woman that he is _____ several times a week.

7. In some cultures where _____ is practiced, the wives live together in the same house, while in others, the husband must establish a separate house for each wife.

8. That silver dish is a family _____ that was given to me by my grandmother.

9. The _____ of his claims to royal blood was proven when it was shown that he was not related to the king or queen at all.

E. Answer the following questions.

1. What does a man in your country do when he wants to court a woman?
2. What are some typical heirlooms in your country?
3. Is polygamy accepted in your country? If so, under what circumstances is it common?
4. Do you think that adultery is common in your country? Why or why not?
5. Are illegitimate children stigmatized in your country? Are there any laws to protect them?
6. Whom do you try to emulate?

WORDS FOR RECOGNITION

KEY WORD	SYNONYMS
beg (v)	beseech, implore, plead
court (v)	woo
dear (adj)	beloved, darling
engaged (adj)	betrothed
family (n)	kin
fascinate (v)	captivate, charm, enchant, enthrall
like (v)	be keen on, dote on, fancy, take to
love (n)	ardor, infatuation
love (v)	adore, cherish
stubborn (adj)	dogged, mulish, obstinate, pertinacious

Example Sentences

beg

He beseeched her not to leave.
He implored her to listen to his request.
She pleaded with her parents to permit her to marry.

court

He has been wooing her for several months.

dear

They watched their beloved grandmother get on the plane.
A picture of his three darling children sat on his desk.

engaged

They became betrothed at an early age, but did not marry until several years later.

family

All of my kin live nearby.

fascinate

She was captivated by his exciting lifestyle.
He was charmed by her gracious manners.
The children were enchanted by the wildlife in the park.
We were enthralled with her stories of her travels.

like

> He is very keen on watching old movies.
> She dotes on her pet dogs.
> Which restaurant do you fancy for dinner tonight?
> She has taken to her new job very quickly.

love (n)

> The depth of her ardor for her boyfriend was visible in her eyes.
> His infatuation with her has lasted for years.

love (v)

> The children adored their aunt and were very sad when she passed away.
> Parents should cherish their children.

stubborn

> A dogged expression came over his face as he refused to answer his mother's
>   question.
> She tends to be mulish when she has made up her mind.
> He can be very obstinate when he thinks he is right.
> She pertinaciously repeated her earlier statement.

Exercises

F.   Circle the word that is least related in meaning.

  1. cherish   beseech   adore
  2. betrothed   darling   beloved
  3. enchant   charm   dote on
  4. mulishness   infatuation   ardor
  5. fancy   woo   court
  6. take to   be keen on   plead
  7. pertinacious   charmed   obstinate
  8. captivate   enthrall   beseech

G.   Write the key word for each set of words.

  1. dogged   mulish   _____
  2. implore   plead   _____
  3. charm   enchant   _____
  4. take to   fancy   _____
  5. ardor   infatuation   _____

      6. be keen on   dote on   _____

      7. enthrall   captivate   _____

      8. cherish   adore   _____

H.   Write the key word that corresponds to each italicized word.

    1. It is not a good idea to *woo* two women at the same time.

    _____

    2. She has been *betrothed* for several weeks. _____

    3. All my *kin* are invited to the wedding. _____

    4. I *beseech* you to reconsider. _____

    5. Don't be so *mulish!* _____

    6. He *is keen on* that idea. _____

    7. Her *ardor* will never diminish. _____

    8. We will always *cherish* these memories. _____

    9. We were *enthralled* by the experience. _____

    10. Let's get married, my *darling*. _____

I.   Write **T** if the sentence is true and **F** if it is false.

    _____ **1.** Some people get betrothed before getting married.

    _____ **2.** A mulish person does not change his or her mind easily.

    _____ **3.** Your kin are related to you.

    _____ **4.** A woman woos a man if she does not like him.

    _____ **5.** When you plead for something you speak against it.

    _____ **6.** People usually only fancy expensive things.

    _____ **7.** People feel infatuation for people that they adore.

    _____ **8.** When a person enthralls you, you think that he or she is pertinacious.

    _____ **9.** Children implore their parents to give them things that they are keen on.

J.   Answer the following questions.

    1. How many living kin do you have?

    2. Do people in your country become formally betrothed before marriage? If so, how long does the period of betrothal usually last?

    3. When you were a child, what did you implore your parents for?

    4. What do you find enchanting?

    5. What do you cherish most about your culture?

    6. What are acceptable ways of wooing a woman in your country?

    7. Do you ever tend to be obstinate? When?

    8. What kind of food do you most often fancy?

Review Exercise for Units 4 and 17

K. In the blanks, write the most appropriate words from the word form charts on pages 29 and 146.

The increase in the number of divorces during the last two decades in the United States has resulted in changes in the way in which many children are being reared. While twenty years ago the mother was almost always given (1) _____ of the children after a divorce, nowadays the decision is often not so clear-cut. Often the court must look very carefully at a particular family in order to decide which (2) _____ will be best able to (3) _____ the children after the divorce. It is indeed a difficult decision, for in many divorce cases in which both parents cherish the children and plead with the court for custody, there is no obvious decision.

The judge in a custody case must take a variety of factors into account in making a decision. The ages of the children is one such factor. When the children are only (4) _____ , the mother is more likely to be given custody. If the children are (5) _____ , and thus able to voice their opinions on which parent they would prefer to live with, the judge often takes their wishes into account. Another factor to be considered is the (6) _____ of each parent. It is generally felt that a parent who has a more even disposition will be better able to avoid major discord when dealing with his or her children.

Overall, the job of the judge who decides custody in a divorce case is to attempt to minimize the friction that is occurring in the lives of the children. The judge must try to make sure that the inevitable (7) _____ which occur during a divorce affect the children as little as possible, and that the children are placed with the parent who is best able to foster their growth and development.

Housing (B)

WORDS FOR PRODUCTION

Word Form Chart

NOUN	VERB	ADJECTIVE
banister		
beam		
boarder	board	boarding
cabin		
chute		
cubicle		
dome		domed
eviction	evict	evicted
fortress		
foyer		
	put up	
squatter	squat	
tile	tile	tiled
tower	tower	towering

Definitions and Examples

1. **banister** [the handrail running alongside a staircase that people hold as they use the stairs]

    Be careful as you go up the stairs! The banister is not secure.

2. **beam** [a long piece of heavy, often squared material such as wood or steel, suitable for construction purposes]

> The framework of the house was constructed of heavy beams.

3. **board** [to pay to stay and receive meals in a home or dormitory]

> She has taken in boarders to earn some money since her husband died.
> You can board in a local home or live in the dormitory while you are studying.
> That is a boarding school, so all of the students live in the dorm.

4. **cabin** [a small, one-story dwelling of simple construction]

> We spend a couple of weeks each summer at our cabin in the woods.

5. **chute** [an inclined channel or passage through which things may pass]

> We put our garbage in that chute, which leads to a collection area in the basement.

6. **cubicle** [a small, partitioned space]

> The office contained one large room and a series of cubicles, each only large enough for one desk and chair.

7. **dome** [a large, hemispherical roof or ceiling]

> Many government buildings in the United States have domes.
> The domed roof of the capital building is made of copper.

8. **evict** [to force a tenant out through legal processes]

> We received an eviction notice and have to leave our apartment by next Friday.
> If you do not pay your rent, you will be evicted.

9. **fortress** [a large, permanent group of buildings which are strongly protected]

> The early settlers in that area had to live in fortresses.

10. **foyer** [an entrance hallway of a home; a lobby of a theater]

> We hung our coats on a rack in the foyer when we entered her house.

11. **put up** (separable) (a) [to construct]

> Many new buildings are being put up right now in this town.

(b) [to give (usually temporary) housing to]

> If you do not have a place to stay, we can put you up for the night.

12. **squat** [to settle on property without right or payment of rent]

> The police are going to evict the squatters from those abandoned houses because they are to be pulled down soon.
> Many homeless people are squatting in that park.

13. **tile** [a flat or curved piece of fired clay, stone, or concrete used especially for roofs, floors, and walls]

> The tile on the walls of the old kitchen was broken in many places.
> We plan on tiling the bathroom floor.
> The house has a red tiled roof.

14. **tower** [a structure that is high relative to its surroundings]

> The mansion has a tower at its northern end.
> The Sears Building towers over the other buildings in downtown Chicago.
> Many people are impressed when they first see the towering Golden Gate Bridge in San Francisco.

Exercises

A. Write **T** if the sentence is true and **F** if it is false.

_____ 1. A boarder lives in his own home.

_____ 2. People often use chutes instead of stairs.

_____ 3. A cubicle is a very small room.

_____ 4. Many homes have a television in the foyer.

_____ 5. A tower is the highest point in a building.

_____ 6. Many bathrooms are tiled.

_____ 7. There are many cabins in urban areas.

_____ 8. Many people have domes in their basements.

_____ 9. The purpose of a fortress is to protect its inhabitants.

_____ 10. People usually want others to squat on their property.

_____ 11. If you do not have a place to stay, you need someone to put you up.

_____ 12. People generally want to avoid being evicted.

B. Answer each question with a word or phrase from the word form chart on page 154.

1. At what kind of school do the children live?
2. What part of a building is a hemisphere?
3. Who is someone who does not have permission to live where he is living?
4. When you enter some homes, what is the first area that you walk through?
5. What do you hold onto when climbing stairs?
6. What may happen to you if you do not pay your rent?
7. What is the tallest part of some buildings?
8. What may cover the floor and walls in a bathroom?
9. What place is well-protected?
10. What do you call a long passage through which things can be dropped or slid?
11. What may the basic structure of a house be made of?

C. Circle the word or phrase that is least related in meaning.

1. room   beam   cubicle
2. put up   board   evict
3. chute   entrance   foyer
4. evict   board   force out
5. tower   stay   squat

D. Complete each analogy with a word or phrase from the word form chart on page 154.

1. curb : street :: _____ : stairs
2. bone : body :: _____ : house
3. lobby : hotel :: _____ : house
4. feed : food :: _____ : shelter
5. divorce : marriage :: _____ : apartment lease
6. cabin : house :: _____ : room

E. In the blanks, write the most appropriate words from the word form chart on page 154.

1. The people used a long, plastic emergency _____ to escape from the burning plane.

2. The elderly woman held onto the _____ tightly as she descended the stairs.

3. There is a large bell in the _____ on the top of the church.

4. The hunters stayed in a wooden _____ during their weeks in the woods.

5. She lives in a _____ house where she receives two meals a day, in addition to a room.

6. He complained to the police that a group of _____ were camping on the edge of his property.

7. The settlers were afraid of Indian attacks, so their homes were more like

   _____ .

8. After not paying their rent for two months, they received a(n)

   _____ notice.

9. The owners of the house agreed to _____ the travelers who were caught in the snowstorm.

10. St. Peter's Basilica in Rome is topped by a large, round _____ .

F. Answer the following questions.

1. Are many of the high schools in your country boarding schools?
2. Do any of the government buildings in your country have domes?
3. Are there squatters in the cities in your country? If so, do the police permit them to stay on the land?
4. Do houses in your country usually have foyers? If so, describe a typical one.
5. Are kitchens or bathrooms usually tiled in your country?
6. Name some buildings in your country that have towers.
7. Do houses in your country ever have exposed beams (on the inside)?

WORDS FOR RECOGNITION

KEY WORD	SYNONYMS
beam (n)	girder, rafter
(small) bed (n)	bunk, cot
bed (for a baby) (n)	cradle, crib
fortress (n)	citadel, stronghold
foyer (n)	vestibule
maintenance (n)	upkeep
pillar (n)	column
room (n)	alcove, chamber

Example Sentences

beam

The building was constructed with large steel girders.
The rafters of the house were visible on the second floor.

(small) bed

The cabins on the ship each contained two bunks.
We asked the hotel manager to put a cot in our room for our daughter to
     sleep on.

bed (for a baby)

The baby in the cradle began to cry.
The crib was next to the parents' bed.

fortress

A large number of soldiers are stationed at the citadel.
The villagers retreated to the stronghold at the first sign of the attack.

foyer

We removed our coats in the vestibule.

maintenance

We are selling our old house because we cannot afford the upkeep for it.

pillar

     The house has four columns across the front.

room

     The house contains several sleeping alcoves.
     Grandfather is spending the evening in his chamber.

Exercises

G.   Circle the word or phrase that is least related in meaning.

     1. girder   stronghold   citadel

     2. foyer   column   vestibule

     3. alcove   cot   bunk

     4. girder   rafter   upkeep

     5. citadel   chamber   alcove

     6. crib   column   cradle

H.   Write the key word for each set of words.

     1. cot   bunk   _____

     2. citadel   stronghold   _____

     3. rafter   girder   _____

     4. cradle   crib   _____

     5. chamber   alcove   _____

I.   Write the key word that corresponds to each italicized word.

     1. A number of *columns* support the front of the roof. _____

     2. The *upkeep* for an older home is more than that for a newer one.

     _____

     3. The owner met us in the *vestibule.* _____

     4. Tell the clerk that we need a *crib* in our room. _____

     5. The *stronghold* is large enough for hundreds of people. _____

     6. The living room of that house has exposed *rafters.* _____

     7. This *bunk* is too hard for me. _____

     8. Rock the *cradle,* and maybe she will fall asleep. _____

     9. This *alcove* will be yours. _____

J.   Write **T** if the sentence is true and **F** if it is false.

_____ 1. Cribs are used by soldiers.

_____ 2. Columns may support the roof of a porch.

_____ 3. A bridge may have steel girders.

_____ 4. The upkeep on an old house may be expensive.

_____ 5. People may sleep in a chamber.

_____ 6. A rafter may contain a cradle.

_____ 7. Soldiers may sleep on cots.

_____ 8. People usually sleep in a vestibule.

_____ 9. A citadel may contain soldiers.

K.   Answer the following questions.

1. Have you ever slept on a cot? If so, when?
2. Does your house have a vestibule?
3. Do people in your country use cradles for infants?
4. Do any of the government buildings in your country have columns? If so, which ones?
5. For what parts of a house in your country is the upkeep most expensive?
6. Does the typical architecture in your country have exposed rafters inside the homes?
7. Are any of the historical places in your country old citadels? Explain.

Review Exercise for Units 5 and 18

L.   Look at the word form charts on pages 37 and 154 and write as many examples of each of the following as you can.

1. types of buildings: _____

2. construction materials: _____

3. types of rooms: _____

4. parts of buildings (excluding rooms): _____

Education and Thought (B)

WORDS FOR PRODUCTION

Word Form Chart

NOUN	VERB	ADJECTIVE	ADVERB
aspiration	aspire	aspiring	
astuteness		astute	astutely
coherence		coherent	coherently
deliberation	deliberate	deliberating	
exasperation	exasperate	exasperated	
		exasperating	
ingenuity		ingenious	ingeniously
intuition	intuit		
prodigy			
	ramble	rambling	
speculation	speculate	speculative	
	squirm		
subtlety		subtle	subtly

Definitions and Examples

1. **aspiration** [a strong desire to achieve something high or great]

    His aspiration is to win a Nobel Prize.
    She aspires to enter law school.
    Many aspiring actors and actresses move to Hollywood.

2. **astute** [combining intelligence, cleverness, and understanding]

> She is known for her astuteness in business matters; that is one reason
> why she is a rich woman.
> If you are astute, you will soon learn how to do well here.
> He astutely asked just the question that I wished to avoid answering.

3. **coherence** [the quality of being connected in a systematic and logical fashion]

> This paragraph is difficult to read because it lacks coherence.
> The accident victim was so upset that his speech was not coherent.
> She coherently described the appearance of the boy who had grabbed her
> purse.

4. **deliberate** [to think about ideas and decisions carefully]

> After much deliberation, she decided to drop out of medical school.
> We cannot give you our decision until we deliberate on this issue.
> The deliberating jury spent several days reviewing the evidence.

5. **exasperate** [to cause irritation or annoyance]

> His exasperation with the delay was evident from the expression on his
> face.
> Students who do not study can really exasperate their teachers.
> The exasperated woman threatened to call the manager if her request was
> not complied with.
> It was exasperating when the pay phone would not work.

6. **ingenuity** [skill or cleverness in devising solutions or combining ideas]

> Everyone admired her ingenuity in solving the problem.
> She came up with an ingenious plan to save the company a lot of money.
> He ingeniously figured out an easier solution to the dilemma.

7. **intuition** [the power of getting direct knowledge without evident rational
thought and inference]

> He says that he makes his business decisions by intuition rather than by
> studying the market situation.
> There is no way that you can intuit this information; you will have to
> research the issue carefully.

8. **prodigy** [a highly talented child]

> Mozart was a prodigy who wrote symphonies when he was only a small
> child.

9. **ramble** [to talk or write in an aimless fashion]

> I do not enjoy her lectures because she rambles so much.
> He took two hours to bring his rambling speech to a close.

10. **speculate** [to think about; to ponder; to guess]

   Scientists have spent many hours in speculation on the origin of the universe.
   It is now necessary to speculate on the meaning of these research results.
   These comments are speculative in nature; as yet we have no firm data.
   (See Unit 10 for another meaning of "speculate")

11. **squirm** [to twist about like a worm]

   The children were tired of sitting for so long and were squirming in their seats.

12. **subtle** [difficult to understand or distinguish]

   The subtlety of his humor is beyond me; I never think that his jokes are funny.
   It is difficult to learn to use words correctly when the differences between them are subtle.
   This wine is subtly sweet.

Exercises

A. Write **T** if the sentence is true and **F** if it is false.

_____ 1. An incoherent person is hard to understand.

_____ 2. People aspire to those things that they wish to avoid in their lives.

_____ 3. Squirming is a sign that someone feels comfortable.

_____ 4. A subtle difference is not very noticeable.

_____ 5. A rambling speech does not get to the point quickly.

_____ 6. An astute person will probably make clever decisions.

_____ 7. It is exasperating to try to teach someone who does not try to learn.

_____ 8. An inventor should not be ingenious.

B. Answer each question with a word from the word form chart on page 162.

1. What should you do before making a decision?
2. What can you call a child who can do advanced math problems?
3. What should you not do while sitting in class?
4. What should a presenter not do during his or her speech?
5. How can you describe a well-organized piece of writing?
6. What kind of point is not easily noticed?
7. What do you have to rely on when making a decision without facts? (two answers)
8. How do you feel when nothing seems to be going well for you?
9. What can you call your dreams of what you hope to do in the future?

C. Circle the word that is least related in meaning.

1. exasperating   aspiring   frustrating
2. rambling   clever   astute
3. connected   subtle   coherent
4. aspiration   objective   intuition
5. aspire   squirm   move
6. subtle   small   large

D. Complete each analogy with a word from the word form chart on page 162.

1. sharp : knife :: _____ : mind
2. plan : action :: _____ : decision
3. torture : pain :: obstacle : _____
4. good : bad :: _____ : obvious
5. crooked : straight :: _____ : direct

E. In the blanks, write the most appropriate words from the word form chart on page 162.

1. I cannot understand this essay because it is not _____ .
2. He _____ to become a veterinarian.
3. After a long period of _____ , they made a decision.
4. It was very _____ of her to realize what the underlying problem was.
5. That is a(n) _____ way to save money.
6. Stop _____ and make your point!
7. Further _____ about the cause of the accident will serve no purpose; we must wait for more facts.
8. The taste of that food is too _____ for me to enjoy it; it seems to me to have no taste.
9. The cat _____ and tried to jump out of my arms.
10. The _____ man screamed at his children to be quiet.

F. Answer the following questions.

1. What do you find to be exasperating?
2. When you make decisions, how much do you rely on intuition?
3. What are your aspirations?
4. Name someone who was or is a prodigy.
5. What do you think is the best way to learn the subtle differences between words in a foreign language?
6. Name someone or something that you think is ingenious.
7. When do you tend to squirm?

WORDS FOR RECOGNITION

KEY WORD	SYNONYMS
astute (adj)	shrewd
astuteness (n)	acumen, discernment
fame (n)	renown
foolish (adj)	absurd, daft
skillful (adj)	accomplished, adept, proficient
spread (v)	disseminate
squirm (v)	fidget
unruly (adj)	clamorous, obstreperous, recalcitrant

Example Sentences

astute

She has made a lot of money because she is a shrewd businesswoman.

astuteness

We admired his acumen during the negotiations.
Her discernment was evident in the way she answered the professor's question.

fame

His renown as a researcher is widespread.

foolish

Many people feel that legalizing drugs like heroin would be absurd.
They think he's daft because he's always talking to himself.

skillful

She is an accomplished pianist although the piano is only her hobby.
The new manager is adept at handling the problems that arise daily.
He is proficient at all the research techniques that you will require of him.

spread

The news of the discovery rapidly disseminated across the community.

squirm

You should try not to fidget while you are waiting.

unruly

> The clamorous behavior of the children has given me a headache.
>
> Her behavior in class is so obstreperous that her teacher has called her parents several times to complain.
>
> He is usually recalcitrant and refuses to do what we ask.

Exercises

G.   Circle the word that is least related in meaning.

1. shrewd   adept   proficient
2. daft   renown   absurd
3. discernment   dissemination   acumen
4. squirm   clamor   fidget
5. daft   obstreperous   recalcitrant
6. accomplished   adept   absurd

H.   Write the key word for each set of words.

1. obstreperous   recalcitrant   _____
2. discernment   acumen   _____
3. accomplished   adept   _____
4. daft   absurd   _____
5. clamorous   obstreperous   _____
6. proficient   adept   _____

I.   Write the key word that corresponds to each italicized word.

1. Stop that *fidgeting!* _____
2. Her *acumen* was obvious. _____
3. She is an *accomplished* liar. _____
4. We are not permitted to *disseminate* any more of that material. _____
5. He is a person of *renown.* _____
6. His behavior tends to be *obstreperous.* _____
7. Joe is a very *adept* musician. _____
8. That is a *daft* idea! _____
9. They are being a bit *recalcitrant.* _____
10. She is quite *shrewd.* _____

J.   Write **T** if the sentence is true and **F** if it is false.

1. Teachers encourage students to be recalcitrant.
2. The purpose of the media is to disseminate information.
3. A person with acumen makes shrewd decisions.
4. A person who is proficient at a foreign language knows that language well.
5. It is good to disseminate absurd ideas.
6. A person with discernment often does daft things.
7. A person may be of renown because he or she is not accomplished at some art.
8. People want to be adept at the things that they do.
9. A bored person may fidget.

K.   Answer the following questions.

1. How is news most often disseminated in your country?
2. How do teachers in your country handle recalcitrant students?
3. Name someone who you feel has great acumen. Explain.
4. What person from your country has the greatest renown worldwide? Explain.
5. At what are you accomplished?
6. How do parents in your country deal with their children when they are obstreperous?
7. Name something that was recently in the news that you felt was daft.
8. How proficient are you at the languages that you have studied?

Review Exercise for Units 6 and 19

L. Look at the word form charts on pages 46 and 162, and list as many words as you can that fit the following specifications.

1. Adjectives that can be used to describe a person's speech: _____

_____

_____

2. Nouns that refer to people: _____

_____

_____

3. Verbs that refer to ways of speaking: _____

_____

_____

4. Nouns that refer to mental activities: _____

_____

_____

Government (B)

WORDS FOR PRODUCTION

Word Form Chart

NOUN	VERB	ADJECTIVE
anarchy		
anarchist		
bureaucracy		bureaucratic
bureaucrat		
consul		
consulate		
deputy	deputize	deputized
fascism		fascist
fascist		
junta		
nobility		
noble		
protocol		
referendum		
regime		
sedition		seditious
subjugation	subjugate	subjugated
totalitarianism		totalitarian

Definitions and Examples

1. **anarchy** [a state of lawlessness or political disorder due to the absence of governmental authority]

   > After the king was overthrown, there was a period of anarchy, during which even the communication and transportation systems across the country did not function.
   >
   > She is an anarchist and speaks out against the government.

2. **bureaucracy** [government characterized by specialization of functions, rigid rules, and a strict hierarchy of authority]

   > Most people dislike dealing with the bureaucracy when they have to get government permission for some action.
   >
   > The system in that country is very bureaucratic: to get anything done, you must get the signatures of at least ten different officials.
   >
   > He is a minor bureaucrat in the government.

3. **consul** [an official appointed by a government to live in a foreign country to represent the commercial interests of his or her home country]

   > She was appointed consul to one of the nations in Southeast Asia.

4. **consulate** [the official residence or office of a consul]

   > We were told that we could obtain that information at the Japanese consulate in Chicago.

5. **deputy** [a second-in-command or assistant who usually takes charge when his or her superior is absent]

   > The consul is out of town, but his deputy will be happy to help you.
   >
   > The police chief deputized several citizens because he lacked sufficient manpower to track the escaped prisoner.
   >
   > The deputized men were sent after the murderer.

6. **fascism** [a political philosophy that places the nation and race above the individual; a centralized government with a dictatorial head and forcible suppression of any opposition]

   > World War II is sometimes referred to as "the war against fascism."
   >
   > The fascist party received few votes in that election.
   >
   > He is a fascist and preaches against democracy.

7. **junta** [a group of persons controlling a government, especially after a revolution]

   > The people are tired of the junta and want elections to be held soon.

8. **nobility** [a small class of people in a society who are privileged because of the family they are born into]

> The members of the nobility used to hold all the power in that country, but now the common people are gaining power.
> The nobles almost always married within their own class.

9. **protocol** [a strict code governing behavior, especially that of diplomats or members of the military]

> In your meeting with the ambassador, you must be careful that protocol is followed.

10. **referendum** [the practice of putting proposed legislation to a popular vote]

> The people are voting today on the referendum concerning income taxes.

11. **regime** [a government in power]

> Many people feel that this regime is not as strong as the last one was.

12. **sedition** [incitement of resistance to or rebellion against lawful authority]

> She was convicted of sedition and exiled.
> Many of his writings are considered to be seditious, so he is not popular with the government.

13. **subjugate** [to force to submit to control or being governed]

> The subjugation of the country that they had invaded took several months.
> The government tried to subjugate the opposition party.
> The subjugated people hated their conquerors.

14. **totalitarian** [of or relating to a political regime based on the subordination of the individual to the state and strict control of all aspects of life]

> She found life under the totalitarian system intolerable.
> The people feared that their conquerors would impose a system of totalitarianism.

Exercises

A.   Write **T** if the sentence is true and **F** if it is false.

_____   **1.** Seditious writing speaks against the regime in a country.

_____   **2.** There is anarchy in a totalitarian state.

_____   **3.** People enjoy dealing with bureaucracies.

_____   **4.** A consul is a type of diplomat.

_____   **5.** A deputy is the top official in an organization.

_____   **6.** In a referendum, only government officials vote.

_____   **7.** The regime in a country changes when the government changes.

_____   **8.** The members of the nobility of a country are usually poor.

_____   **9.** People enjoy being subjugated.

_____   **10.** Protocol is a system of rules.

B.   Answer each question with a word from the word form chart on page 170.

   1. Who is a second-in-command?
   2. Who works for his or her own government, but works in a foreign country?
   3. Who wants to overthrow a government?
   4. What should be followed when diplomats meet?
   5. What do invaders often want to do to the people of the land that they invade?
   6. What group of people rules a country?
   7. Who is of high social class?
   8. What is a type of vote?
   9. What were Hitler and Mussolini examples of?
   10. What word for "government official" has a negative meaning?

C.   Circle the word that is least related in meaning.

   1. referendum   government   regime

   2. treason   sedition   junta

   3. anarchist   consul   diplomat

   4. rules   nobility   protocol

   5. conquer   deputize   subjugate

   6. fascist   official   bureaucrat

   7. vote   referendum   regime

   8. anarchy   fascism   totalitarianism

D. In the blanks, write the most appropriate words from the word form chart on page 170.

1. A(n) _____ consisting of five men took power after the revolution.

2. The meeting dissolved into a series of arguments because many of the participants felt that the proper _____ had not been followed.

3. During the emergency the police chief _____ a number of volunteers to help keep order.

4. That government is _____ in nature, and permits its citizens very little freedom.

5. After the revolution the _____ in that country were stripped of their former power and prestige.

6. That country has been in political turmoil for the past ten years: they have had a series of _____ , each lasting only a few months.

7. The question of whether the legal age for voting should be lowered will be put to a(n) _____ next month; the decision will be in the hands of the voters.

8. They faced a number of _____ delays in their effort to emigrate.

9. If his writings are judged to be _____ , he could be imprisoned.

10. The bomber belonged to a small group of _____ , who were trying to bring chaos to the government system.

E. Answer the following questions.

1. Do any countries have consulates in the city where (or near where) you live?
2. Does your country currently have nobles? Did it have nobility in the past?
3. Does your country have referendums? If so, what did the last one concern?
4. How long has the regime in your country been in office?
5. Has your country ever had a period of anarchy? If so, when?
6. Do you think that your country has a lot of bureaucracy? Explain.
7. Has your country ever been subjugated? Explain.

WORDS FOR RECOGNITION

KEY WORD	SYNONYMS
administer (v)	preside over
announce (v)	proclaim
bribery (n)	graft, payola
conservative (adj)	reactionary
demand (v)	agitate for
order (n)	edict
plot (n)	intrigue
rebel (n)	insurgent
rebel (v)	revolt
rebellion (n)	insurgency, insurrection

Example Sentences

administer

The president presides over the House of Representatives in that country.

announce

The government has proclaimed that the war is over.

bribery

There is too much graft in our government.
His office has been accused of accepting payola.

conservative

That party is reactionary and resists all change.

demand

The people have been agitating for more freedom.

order

The edict concerning the flying of the flag was not well received by the
citizens.

plot

The police have discovered an intrigue to blow up several government
buildings.

rebel (n)

> The insurgents have gained control of a number of small towns.

rebel (v)

> Some parts of the military have revolted and are trying to take control of the government.

rebellion

> The insurgency was quickly put down by the government troops.
> The insurrection led to the establishment of a new regime.

Exercises

F.   Circle the word that is least related in meaning.

1. intrigue   plot   edict
2. revolt   proclaim   announce
3. insurgent   reactionary   conservative
4. insurgency   insurrection   intrigue
5. payola   graft   proclamation
6. agitate for   demand   preside over

G.   Write the key word for each set of words.

1. insurgency   insurrection   _____
2. payola   graft   _____

H.   Write the key word that corresponds to each set of italicized words.

1. They *revolted* against his cruel rule. _____
2. The people are *agitating for* reforms. _____
3. There is a bad *payola* problem in this city. _____
4. The edict was *proclaimed* last night. _____
5. They dismissed her plan as too *reactionary*. _____
6. Their *intrigue* was discovered. _____
7. She is *presiding over* the investigation. _____
8. The *insurgents* are very strong. _____
9. It was a clear case of *graft*. _____
10. Many lives were lost during the *insurrection*. _____

I.   Write **T** if the sentence is true and **F** if it is false.

_____ **1.** Edicts are often proclaimed.

_____ **2.** Bureaucrats should accept payola.

_____ **3.** People agitate for things that they are against.

_____ **4.** Most intrigues are well known to the public.

_____ **5.** Insurgents may participate in an insurrection.

_____ **6.** Reactionary people favor liberal changes.

_____ **7.** The person presiding over a meeting is in charge of it.

_____ **8.** Graft helps a country prosper.

J.   Answer the following questions.

1. Name someone whose views you think are reactionary.
2. Is graft a problem in the local government where you live? Explain.
3. What have the people in your country agitated for in the past?
4. Has there ever been an insurgency in your country? Explain.
5. Describe a recent edict from your government.
6. What part of the government of your country deals with intrigues against the government?

Review Exercise for Units 7 and 20

K. Write the words from the word form charts on pages 55 and 170 that best answer each question.

1. Which nouns refer to political ideologies? _____

_____

_____

2. Which nouns always refer to people who work for a government? _____

_____

_____

3. Which words (two verbs and three nouns) refer to elections? _____

_____

_____

4. Which words can refer to persons? _____

_____

_____

5. Which four verbs refer to negative actions that one group of people can take against another group? _____

_____

_____

Nature (B)

WORDS FOR PRODUCTION

Word Form Chart

NOUN	VERB	ADJECTIVE	ADVERB
aberration		aberrant	aberrantly
abyss			
		barren	
	bloom	blooming	
crevice			
		dormant	
game			
invigoration	invigorate	invigorating	
puddle			
stroll	stroll		
surge	surge	surging	
tide			

Definitions and Examples

1. **aberrant** [being different from the normal, usual, or right away]

    Such warm weather in January is an aberration here since it is usually much colder.

    The aberrant appearance of the bear near their cabin frightened the hunters.

    Animals which behave aberrantly may be diseased.

2. **abyss** [an immeasurably deep place or great space]

   The sides of the abyss were very steep, and we were afraid to go near the edge.

3. **barren** (a) [lacking a normal or adequate covering of vegetation or crops]

   The land was barren because of the drought.

   (b) [incapable of producing offspring]

   Many of the cows are barren now because of the sickness that they suffered last year.

4. **bloom** [to produce or yield flowers]

   The garden is beautiful in the spring when the flowers are blooming.
   The blooming vegetation gave off a heavenly smell.

5. **crevice** [a narrow opening resulting from a crack or split]

   He caught his foot in a crevice in the rock.

6. **dormant** [inactive; asleep; having biological activity suspended]

   These plants go through a dormant stage in the winter but then bloom each spring.

7. **game** [an animal which is hunted]

   The hunters were after a variety of game, including birds and small animals.

8. **invigorate** [to give life and energy to]

   Many people enjoy the invigoration of a walk through the snow.
   I am always invigorated by a cold shower.
   She breathed in the cold, invigorating air deeply.

9. **puddle** [a very small pool of usually dirty or muddy water or another liquid]

   The rain left puddles all over the road.

10. **stroll** [to walk in a leisurely or idle manner]

    I would like to take a stroll on the beach as the sun sets.
    He spends most of the day just strolling around the town.

11. **surge** [to rise and fall actively]

    A surge of a wave got our towels all wet.
    During storms the water sometimes surges right up to the porch.
    They were frightened by the surging waves during the storm.

12. **tide** [the alternate rising and falling of the surface of the ocean (and other bodies of water connected with the ocean) that occurs twice a day and is caused by the gravitational pull of the sun and moon]

>   Now this beach is wide because the tide is out, but at high tide there is only a narrow stretch of dry sand.

Exercises

A. Write **T** if the sentence is true and **F** if it is false.

_____ 1. If you are in a hurry, you do not stroll.

_____ 2. Hunters try to find and kill game.

_____ 3. Snow in Alaska is an aberration.

_____ 4. A barren landscape is usually covered with vegetation.

_____ 5. If you feel invigorated, you need a nap.

_____ 6. An abyss is always deep.

_____ 7. A crevice is always deep.

_____ 8. Plants bloom during their dormant period.

_____ 9. Most rivers have tides.

_____ 10. Rain leaves puddles on streets.

B. Answer each question with a word from the word form chart on page 179.

1. What do ocean waves do during a storm?
2. During what type of phase may a plant seem to be dead?
3. What causes a beach to look different at different times of the day?
4. What kind of behavior will probably surprise people?
5. What is something that can be eaten?
6. What is a good feeling?
7. What do people like to do in parks?
8. What do flowers do in the spring?
9. What is the condition of an animal that cannot have children?

C. Circle the word that is least related in meaning.

1. walk   surge   stroll

2. puddle   crevice   crack

3. game   prey   abyss

4. flower   puddle   bloom

5. barren   aberrant   unusual

6. invigorating   inactive   dormant

D. Complete each analogy with a word from the word form chart on page 179.

    1. animal : prey :: man : _____
    2. good : bad :: normal : _____
    3. pond : ocean :: _____ : abyss
    4. begin : end :: _____ : die
    5. animal: hibernating :: plant : _____
    6. begin : end :: _____ : tire
    7. room : empty :: landscape : _____

E. In the blanks, write the most appropriate words from the word form chart on page 179.

    1. The _____ water reached all the way to where our things were lying on the sand.
    2. We could not see to the bottom of the _____ .
    3. The _____ in the temperature caused many of the crops to die.
    4. The _____ cool air helped to clear my head.
    5. That volcano is not dangerous now because it is _____ .
    6. At high _____ the water here is deep enough to swim in.
    7. The child was all muddy because she had been playing in a(n)

    _____ .

    8. This area is so _____ that no one lives here.
    9. The small animal disappeared into a(n) _____ in the rock.

F. Answer the following questions.

    1. Where do you most like to take strolls?
    2. What types of game do people in your country hunt?
    3. What do you find to be invigorating?
    4. What part of your country is comparatively barren?
    5. When does your favorite flower bloom?
    6. Where have you observed the tides? How much of a difference was there between the water levels at high and low tides?
    7. Describe a type of behavior that is considered aberrant in your culture.
    8. Are there any dormant volcanoes in your country? Are there any active ones?

WORDS FOR RECOGNITION

KEY WORD	SYNONYMS
channel (n)	strait
cave (n)	cavern, grotto
crevice (n)	crevasse, fissure
huge (adj)	colossal, immense, mammoth
peak (n)	pinnacle, summit
plain (n)	prairie, savannah
stroll (v)	amble, saunter
valley (n)	glen, gorge, ravine

Example Sentences

channel

The ships must pass through this narrow strait in order to enter the harbor.

cave

We crawled through the small opening and discovered a cavern.
The small grotto was hardly large enough for us to stand up in.

crevice

The crevasse ran along the face of the cliff.
The rock had a number of fissures, but none of them was wide enough to reach into.

huge

The colossal mountain towered over our heads.
They felt an immense sense of relief when they saw that the little boy was unharmed.
As she had never visited a big city before, she was amazed at the sight of the mammoth buildings.

peak

He is at the pinnacle of his career right now.
They climbed for two days but had to give up before reaching the summit because of the threatening weather.

plain

As we looked across the prairie, no mountain or building disturbed its perfect flatness.
Only tall grass grew on the savannah.

stroll

> He ambled along and appeared to have no particular destination in mind.
> They sauntered about the town, stopping occasionally to look in one of the store windows.

valley

> No sunlight reached the bottom of the glen because of the many trees.
> We went through a steep gorge in order to avoid having to hike over the mountains.
> The child fell over the cliff and rolled all the way to the bottom of the ravine.

Exercises

G. Circle the word that is least related in meaning.

     1. savannah   ravine   prairie

     2. colossal   crevasse   fissure

     3. gorge   grotto   glen

     4. pinnacle   summit   cavern

     5. strait   saunter   amble

     6. mammoth   gorge   immense

     7. grotto   cavern   prairie

H. Write the key word for each set of words.

     1. amble   saunter   _____

     2. pinnacle   summit   _____

     3. colossal   mammoth   immense   _____

     4. fissure   crevasse   _____

     5. gorge   ravine   glen   _____

     6. grotto   cavern   _____

I.   Write the key word that corresponds to each italicized word.

    1. This project has been a *colossal* failure. _____

    2. They *sauntered* into view. _____

    3. The enemy has placed mines in the *strait.* _____

    4. We will reach the *summit* soon. _____

    5. She dropped her camera in a *crevasse* and was unable to reach it.

    _____

    6. It was cool in the *grotto.* _____

    7. That *ravine* looks quite deep. _____

    8. Lions are found on the *savannah.* _____

    9. The *mammoth* ship sank quickly. _____

    10. The *pinnacle* is visible from here. _____

    11. He *ambled* slowly over to us. _____

    12. We could see nothing in the *fissure.* _____

    13. They found him at the bottom of the *gorge.* _____

    14. The problem is *immense.* _____

J.   Write **T** if the sentence is true and **F** if it is false.

    ____ **1.** A fissure is usually immense.

    ____ **2.** A mountain has a summit.

    ____ **3.** A person who is sauntering is not moving fast.

    ____ **4.** A prairie has a pinnacle.

    ____ **5.** A savannah has many gorges.

    ____ **6.** A ravine is the highest point of a mountain.

    ____ **7.** A mountain may contain a cavern.

    ____ **8.** You may amble if you are out walking just for fun.

    ____ **9.** Whales are colossal animals.

    ____ **10.** Ships may pass through a strait.

K.   Answer the following questions.

    1. Have you ever been inside of a cavern? Explain.
    2. Do prairies or savannahs exist in any area of your country? Explain.
    3. Name something that you think is colossal.
    4. How high is the summit of the highest mountain in your country?
    5. Describe a gorge that you have seen.
    6. What do you think can cause fissures to form in rock?
    7. What is the most immense problem that your country currently faces?

Review Exercise for Units 8 and 21

L. In the blanks, write the most appropriate words from the word form charts on pages 64 and 179.

Yesterday, Timothy Brown, age six, was rescued relatively unharmed after spending ten hours trapped in a fissure in the rocks which line Cold Water Beach. The child had wandered away from his parents while taking a(n) (1) _____ along the cliffs. He apparently slipped into the small (2) _____ and was knocked unconscious. His frightened parents frantically searched unsuccessfully for him for more than an hour before deciding to go for help. Because of the (3) _____ of the area of Cold Water Beach, search parties did not arrive and begin work until approximately two hours later.

As the crags along the beach are quite sheer, and at high (4) _____ the water reaches the bottom of the cliffs, the searchers feared that the boy had fallen over the cliff and been carried out to sea by the (5) _____ water. Leaders of the search could not understand how the boy could be on the (6) _____ top of the cliffs and not be visible to them. Several (7) _____ along the precipitous edges of the escarpments were carefully checked, but Timothy remained missing.

Finally, the mystery was solved when one of the searchers heard a(n) (8) _____ cry from below her feet. On investigating the strange sound, she found the boy in a narrow crevasse, invisible to those above. Finally awake, Timothy crawled out to meet his rescuer. His parents report that from now on, Timothy will not leave their sight.

Health (B)

WORDS FOR PRODUCTION

Word Form Chart

NOUN	VERB	ADJECTIVE	ADVERB
anatomy		anatomical	anatomically
asylum			
cramp			
flesh		fleshy	
flush	flush	flushed	
gasp	gasp	gasping	gaspingly
hallucination	hallucinate	hallucinating	
		hallucinogenic	
midwife			
miscarriage	miscarry		
ominousness		ominous	ominously
scalpel			
suffocation	suffocate	suffocated	
		suffocating	
trauma		traumatic	

Definitions and Examples

1. **anatomy** [the structural makeup of an animal]

    Medical students must take a course covering human anatomy.
    There are various anatomical differences between humans and apes.
    Men and women are anatomically different to some degree.

2. **asylum** [an institution for the care of the sick, especially the mentally ill]

   He has spent the last ten years in an asylum after killing his wife.

3. **cramp** [a painful, involuntary contraction of a muscle]

   She drowned when she got a stomach cramp while she was swimming alone.

4. **flesh** [the soft parts of the body of an animal]

   Vegetarians do not eat animal flesh.
   The doctor gave the injection in the fleshy part of her arm.

5. **flushed** [having a reddish color in one's skin]

   A flush spread across her face when she realized she was the object of their joke.
   I flush whenever I am embarrassed.
   The patient's flushed face told the doctor that he was running a fever.

6. **gasp** [to breathe loudly and with difficulty]

   The patient's gasps told the doctor that she was in poor condition.
   He gasped for breath as he climbed the stairs.
   The gasping boy asked the coach to take him out of the game.

7. **hallucinate** [to perceive imaginary things]

   As part of her hallucination, she saw snakes climbing the walls of her room.
   That drug may cause him to hallucinate.
   The hallucinating man jumped off a building because he thought that he had wings.
   The tribe uses hallucinogenic drugs as part of their religion.

8. **midwife** [a woman who assists other women in childbirth]

   She had a midwife help with the birth of her child because she wanted to have the baby at home.

9. **miscarriage** [the involuntary end of a pregnancy before the baby is able to survive outside of the mother's body]

   They were very sad that her first pregnancy ended with a miscarriage during the third month.
   As she had miscarried several times, the doctor advised her not to try to have a child again.

10. **ominous** [indicating the probability of future evil]

    They are trying to ignore the ominousness of the doctor's prediction.
    That cough sounds ominous; you should see a doctor.
    The doctor shook his head ominously as he listened to the old man's heart.

11. **scalpel** [a small, straight knife used in surgery]

    He used several scalpels during the operation.

12. **suffocate** [to deprive of oxygen]

    Suffocation can result if small children play with large plastic bags.
    Take that pillow off your brother's face before he suffocates!
    The rescuers were unable to revive the suffocated little girl.
    The heat in here is suffocating; I can hardly breathe!

13. **trauma** (a) [a wound]

    She suffered a trauma to her head during the game.

    (b) [a disordered behavioral state resulting from mental, emotional, or physical stress]

    The little girl has stopped talking since the accident because of the trauma of seeing her mother killed.
    It will take a while for her to recover from such a traumatic experience.

Exercises

A. Write **T** if the sentence is true and **F** if it is false.

_____ **1.** People are pleased to hear ominous news.

_____ **2.** Midwives try to cause miscarriages.

_____ **3.** A doctor must understand anatomy.

_____ **4.** A person who suffers from hallucinations may have to go to an asylum.

_____ **5.** Using a scalpel will help prevent stomach cramps.

_____ **6.** Exercise causes some people to gasp.

_____ **7.** People often flush when they are embarrassed.

_____ **8.** Almost suffocating may produce trauma in a person.

_____ **9.** A thin person has less flesh than an overweight person.

E. In the blanks, write the most appropriate words from the word form chart on page 187.

    1. That poor woman had two _____ before she gave birth to a healthy baby.

    2. That _____ book gives the name for each of the bones in the body.

    3. She is so thin that she has very little _____ on her bones.

    4. That _____ houses a large number of people who are mentally ill.

    5. You should do stretching exercises before you begin to run in order to avoid _____ in your legs.

    6. The fever gave him a(n) _____ appearance.

    7. That high a fever is a(n) _____ symptom; you should take her to the hospital immediately.

    8. Whenever I have to run, I always end up _____ for breath.

    9. The patient has a severe head _____ and will probably be unconscious for several hours.

    10. Her labor pains have started—the baby must be coming—call the _____ quickly!

F. Answer the following questions.

    1. Do women in your country usually have midwives or doctors deliver their babies? Explain.

    2. What event in your life was traumatic for you?

    3. Do you ever get leg cramps? What do you do when you get one?

    4. What ominous news have you heard recently?

    5. What makes you flush?

    6. Are mentally ill people in your country often placed in asylums? Are the asylums public or private?

WORDS FOR RECOGNITION

KEY WORD	SYNONYMS
bleed (v)	hemorrhage
break (v)	fracture
disappear (v)	vanish
endurance (n)	stamina
fat (adj)	chubby, obese, plump, stout
gasp (v)	pant
prevent (v)	avert, fend off, ward off
suffocate (v)	asphyxiate, smother
tired (adj)	fatigued, weary
weak (adj)	feeble, frail

Example Sentences

bleed

They rushed the patient to the operating room because he was hemorrhaging.

break

Her leg was fractured in the accident.

disappear

Her symptoms mysteriously vanished in a few days although she had received no treatment.

endurance

He did not have enough stamina to work twelve hours a day.

fat

He was chubby as a teenager but later grew to be tall and thin.
Obese people run the risk of various medical problems.
She grew plump as she got older.
He is rather short and stout.

gasp

The runners were panting as they finished the race.

prevent

> The health department officials are quarantining the town to avert the spread of the disease.
> He was too weak to fend off the illness and fell ill.
> People have lots of strange ideas about how to ward off colds.

suffocate

> The victims of the fire were asphyxiated by the smoke.
> He felt smothered by the blanket over his face.

tired

> She should avoid getting fatigued during this period of recovery.
> You look weary; you should get more rest.

weak

> My grandfather is quite feeble now.
> Her illness left her very frail.

Exercises

G. Circle the word or phrase that is least related in meaning.

    1. pant   gasp   plump

    2. fracture   vanish   disappear

    3. frail   fend off   feeble

    4. hemorrhage   avert   bleed

    5. stout   weary   chubby

    6. endurance   stamina   smother

H. Write the key word for each set of words.

    1. feeble   frail   _____

    2. chubby   plump   _____

    3. fend off   ward off   _____

    4. weary   fatigued   _____

    5. smother   asphyxiate   _____

    6. obese   stout   _____

    7. avert   fend off   _____

I. Write the key word that corresponds to each italicized word.

1. The child was accidentally *smothered*. _____
2. He is too *weary* to proceed. _____
3. They were too late to *avert* the deaths of many of the victims. _____
4. That *hemorrhaging* must be stopped. _____
5. The boys were *panting* heavily when they arrived. _____
6. All the symptoms have *vanished*. _____
7. She is *plumper* than her sister. _____
8. She is too *feeble* to walk that distance. _____
9. His *stamina* was not equal to the task. _____
10. Her attempt to *ward off* the illness failed. _____
11. The *fracture* was a bad one. _____
12. They will *asphyxiate* soon if we do not reach them. _____

J. Write **T** if the sentence is true and **F** if it is false.

_____ 1. A person with a lot of stamina gets fatigued easily.
_____ 2. A feeble person cannot ward off disease easily.
_____ 3. Hemorrhaging is a serious symptom.
_____ 4. Exercise may cause a chubby child to pant.
_____ 5. Bones are frequently asphyxiated.
_____ 6. An obese person needs to eat more to become strong.
_____ 7. Very elderly people are often frail.
_____ 8. Surgeons try to avert hemorrhages during operations.
_____ 9. People often vanish when they fend off an illness.

K. Answer the following questions.

1. Do you often feel fatigued? Why or why not?
2. Have you ever fractured a bone? Explain.
3. What do you think is the best way to fend off colds?
4. Is being plump considered to be a good or bad thing in your culture? Explain.
5. Do you think that you have a lot of stamina? Give an example to support your answer.
6. Does running make you pant? Explain.
7. Name something that has vanished during the past 50 years in your country.

Review Exercise for Units 9 and 22

L. Answer the following questions with words from the word form charts on pages 72 and 187.

1. Which three verbs are related to breathing? _____

_____

_____

2. Which two nouns are related to pregnancy? _____

_____

_____

3. Which four nouns are related to the treatment of medical problems? _____

_____

_____

4. Which nine nouns describe possible symptoms of medical problems? _____

_____

_____

5. Which two words refer to tools that might be used in a hospital? _____

_____

_____

Answer Key

Unit 1

A. 1. T 2. T 3. T 4. T 5. T 6. F 7. T 8. F 9. T

B. 1. interrogation/torture 2. felony 3. assassin 4. embezzler
5. misdemeanor 6. torture 7. revenge 8. perjurer 9. alibi 10. assault
11. counterfeit

C. 1. perjure 2. felon 3. embezzle 4. misdemeanor 5. assassinate
6. assault 7. lurk 8. embezzle 9. counterfeit

F. 1. pummel 2. menace 3. weird 4. inmate 5. holler 6. yell

G. 1. secretly 2. prisoner 3. prison 4. prison 5. scream 6. revenge
7. scream

H. 1. screamed 2. revenge 3. lurking 4. attacker 5. secret 6. prisoners
7. scream 8. prison 9. revenge 10. prisoners

Unit 2

A. 1. T 2. F 3. F 4. T 5. F 6. F 7. F 8. T 9. T 10. T 11. F 12. T 13. F

B. 1. tardy 2. botched 3. underling 4. adverse 5. adamantly 6. dawdling
7. inept 8. grueling 9. grim 10. impediment/adversity 11. aimlessly
12. shift

C. 1. dawdle 2. aimless 3. tardy 4. mollified 5. botch 6. supervisor
7. mock 8. adamant 9. aimlessness 10. errand

D. 1. errand 2. botch 3. underling 4. grueling 5. adamant 6. aimless/inept

G. 1. desultory 2. assent 3. ruinous 4. bungle 5. bungle 6. appease

H. 1. impede 2. adverse 3. dawdle 4. diligent 5. adverse 6. mollify 7. grim

I. 1. agreed 2. mollified 3. adverse 4. dawdled 5. grim 6. underlings
7. dawdling 8. botch 9. aimless

Unit 3

A. 1. T 2. T 3. F 4. F 5. F 6. F 7. T 8. T 9. F 10. T

B. 1. loot 2. retaliate 3. deserter 4. siege 5. truce 6. casualty 7. barracks/garrison 8. mercenary 9. civilian 10. ambush

C. 1. civilian 2. ambush 3. raid 4. besiege 5. hostility 6. loot 7. garrison 8. ambush

D. 1. deserter 2. desert 3. barracks 4. camouflage 5. civilian

G. 1. ruse 2. booty 3. pillage 4. spoils 5. sentry 6. foe 7. adversary 8. armistice

H. 1. loot 2. hostility 3. truce 4. enemy 5. raid 6. trick 7. loot 8. surrender

I. 1. guard 2. retaliation 3. raid 4. truce 5. looted 6. trick 7. surrender 8. enemies 9. loot 10. hostility 11. surrendered 12. enemies

Unit 4

A. 1. T 2. T 3. F 4. T 5. F 6. F 7. T 8. F 9. T

B. 1. scold/spank 2. toddler 3. descendants 4. guardian 5. adolescent 6. conflict 7. embrace 8. nurture 9. adopt 10. custody 11. foster

C. 1. descendant 2. ward 3. embrace 4. temperament 5. scold 6. spanking 7. grandfather 8. scold

D. 1. descendant 2. adolescent 3. embrace 4. guardian 5. scold 6. spank

G. 1. sob 2. reprimand 3. stock 4. admonish 5. cuddle 6. rear 7. disposition 8. wail

H. 1. scold 2. embrace 3. conflict 4. cry 5. conflict 6. descent 7. cry 8. scold

I. 1. embraced 2. raised 3. temperament 4. conflict 5. scolded 6. descent 7. crying 8. scolded 9. conflict 10. cried 11. embraced 12. descent

Unit 5

A. 1. T 2. F 3. F 4. T 5. F 6. F 7. T 8. T 9. T 10. F 11. T 12. T

B. 1. partition 2. shed 3. ventilation 4. ghetto/tenement 5. mansion/palace 6. pantry 7. awning 8. lean 9. pillar

C. 1. partition 2. ramp 3. palace 4. remove 5. shed 6. awning 7. disposal

D. 1. ghetto 2. ventilate 3. pantry 4. awning

G. 1. larder 2. loft 3. domicile 4. edifice 5. erect 6. refuge 7. pantry 8. dwelling

H. 1. dirt 2. attic 3. home 4. lean 5. porch 6. home

I. 1. home 2. dirt 3. shelter 4. leaning 5. porch 6. building 7. built 8. attic; dirty 9. pantry 10. attic

Unit 6

A. 1. F 2. T 3. F 4. T 5. F 6. T 7. T 8. T 9. F

B. 1. truant 2. inference 3. apprentice 4. unruliness 5. mumbling
6. discernment/insight 7. retard

C. 1. apprentice 2. retard 3. drawback 4. truancy 5. doctrine 6. apt
7. apprenticed 8. unable

F. 1. murder 2. novice 3. lucid 4. retard 5. notion 6. mutter 7. tenet
8. novice 9. ponder 10. dogma

G. 1. fool 2. think 3. doctrine 4. confuse 5. fool 6. wise

H. 1. clear 2. idea 3. mumble 4. beginner 5. think (about) 6. doctrines
7. confused 8. wise 9. fool 10. awareness

Unit 7

A. 1. F 2. F 3. T 4. F 5. T 6. T 7. T 8. F 9. F 10. T

B. 1. bully 2. exile 3. overthrow 4. prime minister 5. nomination
6. ideology 7. ballot 8. crusader 9. enfranchised 10. persecute/exile
11. treason

C. 1. align 2. exile 3. bully 4. enfranchise 5. overthrow 6. crusader
7. incite 8. jurisdiction

D. 1. ideology 2. nominate 3. tyrant 4. exile 5. ballot 6. incite

G. 1. abet 2. subvert 3. prerogative 4. treachery 5. abrogate 6. foment
7. president

H. 1. revoke 2. incite 3. scheme 4. revoke 5. consequence 6. incite

I. 1. overthrow 2. right 3. cut 4. treason 5. prime minister
6. consequences 7. revoked 8. inciting 9. scheme 10. incites

Unit 8

A. 1. F 2. T 3. F 4. F 5. F 6. T 7. T 8. T. 9. F 10. T 11. F 12. F

B. 1. prey 2. avalanche 3. ledge 4. hermit 5. mist 6. clearing 7. ditch
8. amphibian 9. scavenger 10. pursue/stalk 11. fierce/predatory

C. 1. amphibian 2. fierce 3. pursue 4. ditch 5. roam 6. scavenge
7. aquatic 8. eerie

D. 1. fierce 2. prey 3. roam 4. avalanche 5. stalk 6. scavenge

G. 1. imperil 2. glade 3. brook 4. ferocious 5. gully 6. trench 7. creek
8. spring 9. brook

H. 1. steep 2. stream 3. ditch 4. jump 5. swamp

I. 1. jeopardize 2. swamp 3. stream 4. clearing 5. fierce 6. cliff
7. ditch 8. jumped 9. swamp 10. ditch 11. cliff 12. stream

Unit 9

A. 1. T   2. F   3. T   4. T   5. F   6. F   7. F   8. T   9. F

B. 1. paralysis   2. bandage/ointment   3. choke   4. coma   5. nausea
    6. numbness   7. stretcher   8. plague   9. revive

C. 1. numbness   2. immune   3. paralysis   4. revived   5. chronic
    6. nauseated   7. revived by

F. 1. queasy   2. feign   3. drowsy   4. vertigo   5. perilous   6. onset   7. feign
    8. pretend   9. onset

G. 1. thin   2. die   3. pill   4. handicapped   5. disease   6. die   7. handicapped
    8. thin

H. 1. sleepy   2. dizziness   3. nauseated   4. pretending   5. beginning
    6. dangerous   7. recovering   8. bandage   9. thin   10. disease   11. pills
    12. died

Unit 10

A. 1. T   2. T   3. F   4. T   5. T   6. F   7. T   8. F   9. T   10. 5

B. 1. voucher   2. auction   3. pawnshop   4. foreclose   5. speculator   6. share
    7. deficit   8. revenue   9. overdue   10. bankrupt/insolvent

C. 1. outlay   2. speculate   3. thrifty   4. foreclose   5. deficit   6. pawned
    7. voucher

F. 1. put on   2. gem   3. frugal   4. defray   5. put aside   6. gem   7. frugal

G. 1. poor   2. trade   3. save   4. poor

H. 1. jewel   2. deal   3. bankrupt   4. greed   5. thrifty   6. pay   7. poor
    8. trade   9. saved   10. poor

Unit 11

A. 1. F   2. T   3. T   4. F   5. F   6. T   7. T   8. F

B. 1. cuff   2. hem   3. seamstress/tailor   4. rinse   5. fastener
    6. mannequin   7. bleach   8. lining   9. ostentatious   10. creased

C. 1. hem   2. crease   3. pleat   4. bleach   5. line   6. cuff   7. rack

D. 1. crease   2. ostentatious   3. rack   4. zipper   5. lining   6. tailor   7. sole
    8. bleach

G. 1. tattered   2. dirty   3. stitch.   4. castoff   5. garish   6. penchant   7. scrub
    8. gaudy

H. 1. preference   2. clean   3. clothing   4. flashy   5. undress   6. preference

I. 1. ugly   2. foam   3. hand-me-downs   4. creased   5. ripped   6. examined
    7. sew   8. flashy   9. clean   10. clothing   11. beautiful   12. undressed

Unit 12

A. 1. F 2. F 3. T 4. T 5. T 6. F 7. T 8. T 9. T 10. T 11. T 12. F

B. 1. delete 2. absurd 3. caustic 4. hint 5. stuttering 6. hoax
7. distorted 8. painstakingly 9. fascade 10. incisive

C. 1. incisive 2. delete 3. blurry 4. interior 5. stutter 6. absurd
7. facade 8. vehement

D. 1. stutter 2. facade 3. distortion 4. delete 5. vehement 6. lurid
7. caustic

G. 1. skeptical 2. garbled 3. reckon 4. delve 5. stammer 6. glimpse
7. henceforth 8. garbled

H. 1. relevant 2. spread 3. hint 4. find out

I. 1. dug 2. lurid 3. from now on 4. started 5. stuttered 6. spread
7. hints 8. find out 9. think 10. said 11. confused 12. doubting

Unit 13

A. 1. T 2. T 3. F 4. F 5. F 6. T 7. T 8. F 9. T 10. F

B. 1. craving 2. intoxicated 3. hoard 4. stale 5. sauce 6. grind
7. abstain/fast 8. shred 9. ration 10. staple 11. gorging

C. 1. abstention 2. spoil 3. grind 4. staple 5. fasting 6. abstain 7. spoil

D. 1. stale 2. crave 3. sober 4. staple 5. ration 6. abstain/fast 7. intoxicate

G. 1. imbibe 2. ravenous 3. banquet 4. blend 5. munch 6. devour
7. tainted 8. dice

H. 1. chew 2. bar 3. chop

I. 1. hungry 2. contaminated 3. bar 4. feast 5. chewed 6. chopped
7. mix 8. drinks 9. ate 10. chew

Unit 14

A. 1. T 2. T 3. F 4. T 5. T 6. T 7. F 8. F 9. F 10. F

B. 1. thwart 2. riot 3. strangler 4. malice 5. evade 6. intimidation
7. rape 8. blackmail 9. incriminate

C. 1. malice 2. molest 3. torture 4. rape 5. ordeal 6. riot 7. blackmail
8. incriminating

F. 1. arraign 2. irked 3. indict 4. assailant 5. skulk 6. dispute 7. dispute

G. 1. charge 2. beat 3. anger 4. argue 5. annoy 6. awful 7. malice
8. awful 9. anger

H. 1. anger 2. annoyed 3. blackmail 4. charged with 5. awful 6. beaten
7. theft 8. escape 9. argument

Unit 15

A. **1.** T **2.** F **3.** F **4.** F **5.** F **6.** F **7.** T **8.** T **9.** T **10.** F

B. **1.** incentive **2.** delegate **3.** ingenuity **4.** hazard **5.** meager **6.** petty
7. picket **8.** strenuous **9.** foreboding

C. **1.** menial **2.** incentive **3.** tardy **4.** delegate **5.** meager **6.** hazardous
7. pettiness **8.** menial

G. **1.** incentive **2.** gain **3.** somber **4.** burly **5.** gripe **6.** petty **7.** terse

H. **1.** brief **2.** muscular **3.** try **4.** meager **5.** hazardous **6.** complain
7. foreboding

I. **1.** brief **2.** hazardous **3.** forebodings **4.** complaining **5.** meager
6. supervisor **7.** complaints **8.** meager **9.** try **10.** muscular

Unit 16

A. **1.** F **2.** F **3.** T **4.** T **5.** F **6.** T **7.** T **8.** F **9.** F **10.** T **11.** T

B. **1.** detonator **2.** martyr **3.** torpedo **4.** partisan **5.** obliterate
6. projectiles **7.** quarters **8.** salute **9.** belligerence **10.** cowed
11. onslaught

C. **1.** martyr **2.** partisans **3.** cow **4.** subside **5.** debris **6.** infringement
7. salute

D. **1.** obliterate **2.** detonate **3.** onslaught **4.** martyr **5.** projectile **6.** quarters

G. **1.** daunt **2.** comply **3.** conscript **4.** taper **5.** detest **6.** rubble **7.** detest

H. **1.** hate **2.** defeat **3.** cautious **4.** die **5.** belligerent **6.** infringe

I. **1.** group **2.** cowed **3.** obeyed **4.** debris **5.** meeting **6.** belligerent
7. draft **8.** infringed **9.** died **10.** cautious **11.** subside **12.** defeated

Unit 17

A. **1.** T **2.** T **3.** F **4.** F **5.** T **6.** F **7.** F **8.** F **9.** T

B. **1.** monogamous **2.** spouse **3.** adultery **4.** illegitimate **5.** clan
6. heirloom **7.** polygamous **8.** suitor **9.** emulation

C. **1.** emulate **2.** illustrative **3.** suitor **4.** seduction **5.** court **6.** suitor
7. monogamous

F. **1.** beseech **2.** betrothed **3.** dote on **4.** mulishness **5.** fancy **6.** plead
7. charmed **8.** beseech

G. **1.** stubborn **2.** beg **3.** fascinate **4.** like **5.** love **6.** like **7.** fascinate
8. love

H. **1.** court **2.** engaged **3.** family **4.** beg **5.** stubborn **6.** likes **7.** love
8. love **9.** fascinated **10.** dear

Unit 18

A. 1. F   2. F   3. T   4. F   5. T   6. T   7. F   8. F   9. T   10. F   11. T   12. T

B. 1. boarding   2. dome   3. squatter   4. foyer   5. banister   6. eviction
7. tower   8. tile   9. fortress   10. chute   11. beams

C. 1. beam   2. evict   3. chute   4. board   5. tower

D. 1. banister   2. beam   3. foyer   4. put up   5. eviction   6. cubicle

G. 1. girder   2. column   3. alcove   4. upkeep   5. citadel   6. column

H. 1. bed   2. fortress   3. beam   4. bed   5. room

I. 1. pillars   2. maintenance   3. foyer   4. bed   5. fortress   6. beams   7. bed
8. bed   9. room

Unit 19

A. 1. T   2. F   3. F   4. T   5. T   6. T   7. T   8. F

B. 1. deliberate   2. prodigy   3. squirm   4. ramble   5. coherent   6. subtle
7. intuition/speculation   8. exasperated   9. aspiration

C. 1. aspiring   2. rambling   3. subtle   4. intuition   5. aspire   6. large

D. 1. astute   2. deliberation   3. exasperation   4. subtle   5. rambling

G. 1. shrewd   2. renown   3. dissemination   4. clamor   5. daft   6. absurd

H. 1. unruly   2. astuteness   3. skillful   4. foolish   5. unruly   6. skillful

I. 1. squirming   2. astuteness   3. skillful   4. spread   5. fame   6. unruly
7. skillful   8. foolish   9. unruly   10. astute

Unit 20

A. 1. T   2. F   3. F   4. T   5. F   6. F   7. T   8. F   9. F   10. T

B. 1. deputy   2. consul   3. anarchist   4. protocol   5. subjugate   6. junta
7. noble/nobility   8. referendum   9. fascists   10. bureaucrat

C. 1. referendum   2. junta   3. anarchist   4. nobility   5. deputize   6. fascist
7. regime   8. anarchy

F. 1. edict   2. revolt   3. insurgent   4. intrigue   5. proclamation   6. preside over

G. 1. rebellion   2. bribery

H. 1. rebelled   2. demanding   3. bribery   4. announced   5. conservative
6. plot   7. administering   8. rebels   9. bribery   10. rebellion

Unit 21

A. 1. T   2. T   3. F   4. F   5. F   6. T   7. F   8. F   9. F   10. T

B. 1. surge   2. dormant   3. tide   4. aberrant   5. game   6. invigoration
7. stroll   8. bloom   9. barren

C. 1. surge   2. puddle   3. abyss   4. puddle   5. barren   6. invigorating

D. 1. game   2. aberrant   3. crevice   4. bloom   5. dormant   6. invigorate
7. barren

B. Answer each question with a word from the word form chart on page 187.

1. Who may help with the birth of a baby?
2. What do you do when you can't catch your breath?
3. What is a surgeon's tool?
4. What part of an animal can be eaten?
5. What would you do without air?
6. What can some drugs cause you to have?
7. What may you get in your leg when you are running?
8. What is one way that a pregnancy may end?
9. What kind of experience is difficult to forget?
10. What changes the color of a person's face?
11. What must medical students study?
12. What kind of prediction are people afraid of?

C. Circle the word that is least related in meaning.

1. skin   flesh   cramp
2. hallucinate   choke   suffocate
3. knife   trauma   scalpel
4. anatomy   institution   asylum
5. pain   cramp   flush
6. gasp   breathe   flesh
7. trauma   anatomy   wound

D. Complete each analogy with a word from the word form chart on page 187.

1. carpenter : hammer :: surgeon : _____
2. good : bad :: favorable : _____
3. food : starve :: air : _____
4. white : black :: pale : _____

G. **1.** ravine **2.** colossal **3.** grotto **4.** cavern **5.** strait **6.** gorge **7.** prairie

H. **1.** stroll **2.** peak **3.** huge **4.** crevice **5.** valley **6.** cave

I. **1.** huge **2.** strolled **3.** channel **4.** peak **5.** crevice **6.** cave **7.** valley
   8. plain **9.** huge **10.** peak **11.** strolled **12.** crevice **13.** valley **14.** huge

Unit 22

A. **1.** F **2.** F **3.** T **4.** T **5.** F **6.** T **7.** T **8.** T **9.** T

B. **1.** midwife **2.** gasp **3.** scalpel **4.** flesh **5.** suffocate **6.** hallucinations
   7. cramp **8.** miscarriage **9.** traumatic **10.** flush **11.** anatomy **12.** ominous

C. **1.** cramp **2.** hallucinate **3.** trauma **4.** anatomy **5.** flush **6.** flesh
   7. anatomy

D. **1.** scalpel **2.** ominous **3.** suffocate **4.** flushed

G. **1.** plump **2.** fracture **3.** fend off **4.** avert **5.** weary **6.** smother

H. **1.** weak **2.** fat **3.** prevent **4.** tired **5.** suffocate **6.** fat **7.** prevent

I. **1.** suffocated **2.** tired **3.** prevent **4.** bleeding **5.** gasping **6.** disappeared
   7. fatter **8.** weak **9.** endurance **10.** prevent **11.** break **12.** suffocate

Combined Index
Words in Volumes 1–6

Numbers refer to **volume** and unit. When an entry has no numbers following it, the word is one of the approximately 600 words assumed for Volume 1. (For separate volume lists, refer to appendices and indexes in Volumes 1–5.)

ago
agony, **6**-17
agree(ment), **3**-18
agriculture, **2**-13
ahead, **5**-14
aid, **4**-12
aim, **5**-8
air
air force, **1**-18
airmail, **3**-5
airplane, **1**-2
airport, **1**-2
alarm, **4**-15
alcohol, **4**-16
alcoholism, **4**-16
alert, **3**-9
alien, **5**-22
alike, **5**-17
alive, **3**-19
all
allergy, **5**-23
allow, **1**-8
ally, **6**-18
almost
almost, **3**-1
alone, **2**-5
along, **4**-24
aloud, **3**-22
already
also
alter, **3**-4
alternate, **6**-15
although, **3**-14
altitude, **3**-8
always
amateur, **3**-21
amaze, **4**-20
ambassador, **1**-20
ambiguous, **5**-24
ambition, **1**-14
ambulance, **1**-16
amend, **4**-1
ammunition, **6**-20
among, **2**-5
amount, **3**-15
ample, **6**-6
amusement, **2**-23
an
analyze, **5**-12
ancestor, **4**-18
anchor, **6**-8
ancient, **2**-22
and
anesthetic, **6**-17

angel, **4**-20
anger, **3**-14
angle, **4**-2
animal
ankle, **3**-19
anniversary, **2**-5
announce, **3**-24
annoy, **5**-10
annual, **2**-2
anonymous, **6**-12
another
answer
anthropology, **5**-5
anticipate, **5**-2
antidote, **6**-17
antique, **4**-7
any
anybody
anyone
anything
anywhere
apartment, **1**-3
apology, **3**-18
apparatus, **5**-5
apparent, **5**-2
appeal, **6**-12
appear(ance), **3**-4
appendix, **6**-10
appetite, **3**-15
applause, **5**-18
apple
application, **5**-14
applied, **6**-7
apply, **1**-1
appoint, **4**-3
appreciate, **6**-9
approach, **5**-1
appropriate for, **2**-9
approve (of), **3**-14
approximately, **2**-22
April
arbitration, **6**-16
architect, **6**-13
are
area, **2**-3
area, **5**-12
argue, **3**-2
arise, **6**-4
arm
arms
arms, **5**-9
army, **1**-18
around, **1**-19
arrange, **5**-22

arrangement, **2**-22
arrest, **2**-7
arrive
arson, **5**-21
article, **2**-17, **5**-25
artificial, **6**-3
artist, **1**-14
as
as a rule, **6**-14
ash, **5**-21
ashamed, **4**-9
ask
aspect, **4**-21
assemble, **4**-16
assembly, **4**-16
assess, **6**-16
asset, **4**-22
assign, **3**-24
assign(ment), **1**-8
assist, **3**-24
associate, **5**-13
association, **5**-13
assume, **4**-23, **5**-18
astonish, **6**-8
astronomy, **2**-24
at
at least, **2**-22
at once, **3**-2
athletic, **3**-23
atlas, **6**-10
atmosphere, **3**-10
atom, **4**-13
attached, **3**-16
attack, **2**-7
attain, **4**-25
attempt, **1**-1
attend, **3**-22
attention (pay), **3**-1
attic, **5**-6
attitude, **3**-7, **4**-1
attract(ive), **4**-10
audience, **1**-9
august
aunt
aunt, **2**-5
authentic, **6**-3
author, **2**-17
authority, **4**-12
automatic, **5**-8
automobile, **1**-2
autonomous, **6**-1
available, **2**-3
avenue, **2**-25
average, **3**-1

dilemma, **5**-22
dilute, **6**-7
dimension, **4**-13
dine, **5**-11
diner, **5**-11
dinner
direct, **5**-8
direction, **1**-21
dirty
disagree with, **5**-23
disappear, **1**-22
disaster, **5**-19
discharge, **6**-20
discipline, **5**-9
discourage, **4**-18
discover, **2**-18
discriminate, **6**-18
discriminating, **6**-18
discuss, **3**-14
disease, **2**-6
disgust, **4**-9
dish, **3**-15
disillusion, **6**-8
disintegrate, **6**-19
dismiss, **3**-24
displace, **6**-13
display, **6**-23
dissolve, **6**-7
distance (long), **1**-24
distill, **6**-24
distinct, **5**-16
distress, **6**-12
distribute, **5**-1
district, **4**-7
disturb, **4**-7
divest, **3**-5
divide, **4**-2
divorce, **2**-5
do
do away with, **6**-15
do over, **5**-8
do without, **5**-18
do without, **6**-3
doctor
document, **4**-12
dog
dollar
domestic, **5**-22
dominant, **6**-21
dominate, **6**-21
door
dormitory
dormitory, **1**-1
dot, **6**-10

double, **3**-17
doubt, **4**-15
down
down payment, **3**-13
dozen, **3**-15
draft, **6**-18
drag, **4**-24
drain, **5**-7
drainage, **5**-7
drama(tic), **2**-23
drastic, **5**-1
draw, **4**-7
draw up, **6**-1
dream
drench, **5**-21
dress, **1**-17
dress up, **5**-15
dress down, **6**-20
drill, **3**-6
drill, **5**-5
drink
drive
drop, **2**-24
drop, **5**-1
drop in, **5**-17
drop out, **5**-5
drown, **4**-6
drug, **5**-1
dry, **1**-4
due, **3**-16
due, **3**-25
dull, **1**-25
dull, **6**-2
dump, **6**-19
durable, **6**-6
duration, **6**-6
during
dust, **3**-16
duty, **3**-20
dwell on, **5**-6
dwelling, **5**-6
dye, **4**-10
dynamic, **6**-8

each
eager, **3**-24
ear
early, **1**-4
earn, **2**-12
earth, **1**-23, **5**-7
earthquake, **4**-8
east
easy

eat
eat up, **6**-3
echo, **4**-4
ecology, **5**-14
economical, **5**-5
economics, **5**-5
economize, **5**-5, **6**-3
economy, **5**-5, **6**-6
edge, **1**-11
edit, **4**-5
educate, **2**-1
effect, **5**-2
efficient, **2**-20
effort, **2**-2
egg
eight
elderly, **4**-18
elect, **2**-11
electricity, **1**-3
element, **6**-19
elementary, **6**-16
elementary school, **1**-1
elements, **6**-19
elephant
elevator, **3**-16
eleven
eliminate, **4**-9
else, **1**-25
embarrassed, **3**-9
embassy, **1**-20
emerge, **6**-25
emergency, **1**-24
emigrate, **4**-12
emit, **5**-12
emotion, **3**-14
emphasis, **3**-7
empire, **6**-18
empirical, **6**-24
employ(ee), **1**-5
empty, **1**-2
enable, **6**-22
enclose, **5**-16
encourage, **4**-18
end
endless, **3**-8
endure, **6**-13
enemy, **1**-18
energy, **4**-6
enforce, **5**-25
engage in, **6**-16
engine, **2**-10
engineering, **2**-19
engulf, **6**-19
enjoy, **1**-7

hesitate, 2-22
hide, 4-15
high
high school, 1-1
highway, 4-24
hill, 1-23
him
himself
hinder, 6-11
hint, 6-10
hire, 2-2
his
history, 2-19
hit
hit on 5-12
hobby, 1-9
hold
hold, 3-15
hold off, 6-1
hold out, 6-20
hold up, 5-25
hole, 3-3
holiday
holy, 3-22
home
honest/honor, 1-20
hook, 6-8
hope
horizon, 5-3
horizontal, 5-3
horn, 1-11
horrible, 1-18
horse
hose, 5-5
hospital
hostility, 6-20
hot
hotel
hour
house
how
however, 3-1
human, 3-9
humble, 5-4
humid, 3-11
hundred
hunger, 2-4
hunt, 3-17
hurricane, 5-16
hurry, 1-11
hurt, 1-16
husband
hut, 6-11

hydroelectric, 6-24
hygiene, 6-17
hypothesis, 5-12

I
ice
idea
ideal, 2-25
identical, 2-5
identify, 4-15
idle, 5-18
if
ignite, 6-25
ignorance, 6-2
ignore, 3-11
ill, 1-16
illuminate, 4-13
illusion, 6-8
illustration, 4-5
image, 6-10
imaginary, 6-25
imagine, 2-23, 6-25
immature, 4-18
immediately, 3-17
immigrate, 4-12
immortal, 4-20
impact, 5-19
impersonal, 1-24
impertinent, 5-24
implement, 6-9
imply, 4-5
import, 3-18
important
impossible, 2-20
impress, 5-24
improve, 2-3
in
in force, 6-20
incendiary, 5-21
incentive, 4-25
inch, 3-19
incident, 4-15
inclination, 6-16
include, 3-11
income, 4-3
inconvenient, 2-3
incorrect, 2-19
increase, 3-2
incredible, 3-10
indefinitely, 4-9
independent, 3-14
index, 4-5

indicate, 5-3
indignant, 6-12
indispensable, 5-8
individual, 2-14
indoors, 1-10
induce, 6-24
industrious, 6-23
industry, 2-20
inefficient, 2-20
infection, 4-6
infinite, 6-24
inflation, 3-25
influence, 3-22
inform, 2-11
ingredient, 5-11
inhabit, 5-18
inherent, 6-21
inherit, 4-7
initially, 3-24
initiate, 2-22, 6-16
initiative, 6-16
injection, 5-2
injury, 2-6
ink, 5-15
innocent, 4-15
input, 6-7
inquire, 5-10
inquiry, 5-10
insane, 5-23
insect, 1-21
insecticide, 6-19
inside
inside, 3-23
insignificant, 4-5
insist, 4-12
inspect, 3-3
install, 5-6
instance, 6-25
instead, 2-10
institute, 5-22
instruct(or), 3-1
instrument, 1-24
insulate, 5-6
insure, 1-13
integrate, 6-4
integrity, 6-21
intellectual, 6-2
intelligent, 2-19
intend, 3-8
intense, 5-20, 6-24
interaction, 6-11
interest
interest, 2-12

interfere, **6**-5
interior, **2**-21, **3**-16
intermediate, **4**-1
internal, **6**-18
international, **2**-11
interpret, **5**-4
interrupt, **5**-24
intersection, **1**-11
interval, **6**-5
intervene, **6**-19
interview, **1**-5
intimate, **6**-5
into
introduce, **4**-9
invade, **3**-20
invent, **2**-16
invest, **4**-22
investigate, **2**-7
invisible, **5**-12
invitation, **1**-13
involve, **5**-10
iron, **3**-10, **4**-2
irrelevant, **5**-24
irrigate, **3**-17
irritate, **5**-14
is
island, **3**-11
isolate, **4**-13
issue, **4**-5
it
item, **1**-13
its
itself
ivory, **5**-16

jacket, **1**-17
jail, **1**-22
jar, **4**-16
jealous, **3**-14
jet, **4**-2
jewel, **4**-25
job
join, **3**-20
joke, **1**-25
journal, **4**-5
journey, **3**-3
joy, **2**-5
judge, **2**-7
juice, **1**-15
jump, **2**-14
jungle, **1**-23
junior, **2**-19, **5**-9
junk, **6**-13

jury, **4**-15
just, **5**-22
justify, **6**-4
juvenile, **5**-25

keep, **3**-15
keep on, **5**-16
keep up with, **6**-2
key
kick, **2**-14
kidnap, **5**-10
kill, **1**-18
kilogram
kilometer
kind, **2**-10, **3**-23
king
kiss
kiss, **3**-14
kitchen
knee, **3**-19
knife
knock, **3**-16
knot, **4**-17
know
knowledge, **4**-1

label, **4**-14
labor, **3**-2
laboratory, **3**-23
lack, **2**-13
ladder, **4**-3
lady
lake, **3**-11
lamb, **4**-16
land
land, **4**-2
landlord/lady, **1**-3
lane, **1**-11
language
large
last
last, **1**-7
late
lately, **5**-2
latitude, **5**-3
laugh
lawn, **1**-12
lawyer, **1**-14
lay, **3**-16
lay in, **5**-9
layer, **3**-6
lazy, **2**-2

lead, **2**-10
leaf, **2**-18
league, **4**-21
leak, **2**-16
lean, **6**-18
learn
lease, **1**-12, **5**-18
leather, **1**-17
leave, **1**-7
leave out, **5**-24
lecture, **3**-1
left
legal, **3**-9
leg
leisure, **4**-25
lend, **2**-12
less, **2**-2
lesson
let, **3**-14
let down, **5**-15, **6**-21
let out, **5**-15, **6**-17
let up, **5**-3
letter
level, **2**-1
lever, **6**-7
liberal, **5**-1
liberty, **3**-18
library
license, **1**-14
lid, **2**-4
lie, **2**-7
lie down, **6**-20
lieutenant, **4**-17
life
lift, **2**-14
light, **1**-13
light, **1**-3, **1**-13
light up, **5**-21
lightning, **3**-11
like
likely, **4**-8
limit, **1**-13
line, **3**-23
liquid, **2**-15
list, **4**-5
listen
literature, **3**-1
little
live
live down, **5**-20
live on, **5**-11
live up to, **6**-21
livestock, **5**-7
load, **3**-3

loan, **4**-22
lobby, **1**-21
local, **1**-24
location, **2**-3
lock, **2**-7
logical, **2**-24
lonely, **2**-22
long
longitude, **5**-3
look
look after, **5**-7
look back on, **5**-7
look down on, **6**-21
look forward to, **5**-13
look into, **5**-10
look over, **5**-8
look up, **5**-24
look up to, **5**-20
loose, **3**-4
Lord, **4**-20
lose/loss, **1**-10
lot, **6**-13
loud, **2**-10
lousy, **5**-3
love
low, **1**-14
loyal, **3**-20
luck, **3**-24
luggage, **1**-7
lunch
lungs, **4**-6
luxury, **4**-4

machine
mad, **3**-21
magazine
magic, **3**-12
magnet, **6**-24
magnitude, **6**-25
maid, **1**-14
mail
main, **4**-2
maintenance, **4**-7
major, **2**-16, **2**-19, **5**-9
majority, **3**-18
make (made)
make out, **6**-7, **6**-14
make up, **5**-13, **5**-17, **6**-16
male
male, **5**-23
mammal, **6**-7
man (men)
manager, **2**-25

mankind, **4**-13
manner, **6**-11
manners, **6**-11
manual, **4**-25
manufacture, **3**-2
many
map
march, **2**-8
marine, **3**-10
mark, **4**-6
mark (grade), **4**-23
market, **2**-13
marry
mass, **3**-10
master, **4**-23
match, **3**-21, **5**-21
material, **2**-9
maternal, **6**-5
mathematics, **2**-19
matter, **4**-22, **6**-10
mature, **6**-5
maximum, **3**-13
may
maybe
mayor, **5**-1
me
mean
mean, **5**-5
mean to, **5**-18
means, **5**-5
measure, **2**-15, **5**-1
meat
mechanic, **6**-7
mechanical, **6**-7
media, **2**-17
medicine
medium, **5**-6
meet
melody, **6**-8
melt, **2**-15
member, **2**-5
memorial, **4**-17
memorize, **4**-17
memory, **4**-17
menace, **5**-22
mental, **3**-12
mention, **5**-4
merchant, **4**-14
mercy, **6**-21
merely, **6**-22
merit, **6**-16
message, **1**-24
meter
method, **2**-16

metric, **3**-10
middle, **1**-11
midnight, **1**-22
might
migrant, **6**-15
mild, **4**-8
mile, **3**-5
military, **1**-18
milk
mill, **6**-15
million
million, **3**-5
mind, **3**-23, **3**-11
mine, **4**-9
minimum, **3**-13
minister, **6**-18
minority, **3**-18
minus, **4**-13
minute
miracle, **3**-22
mirror, **1**-17
miserable, **6**-13
Miss
miss, **2**-1
missile, **6**-20
mission, **6**-21
mistake
misuse, **5**-14
mix, **5**-11
mobility, **5**-18
model, **3**-12
moderate, **6**-6
modern, **2**-10
modest, **3**-21
modify, **6**-23
moist, **5**-3
monetary, **6**-14
money
monopolize, **6**-16
monopoly, **6**-16
month
monthly, **2**-2
mood, **5**-2
moon
moral, **5**-21
morals, **5**-21
more
moreover, **6**-23
morning
mortal, **4**-20
most
motel, **1**-7
mother
motion, **4**-2

motive, 5-25
motor, 3-3
mount, 6-11
mountain
mouth
move
move, 1-11
movement, 6-4
movies
Mr.
Mrs.
much
mud, 1-23
multiply, 2-12
municipal, 6-1
murder, 1-22
muscle, 4-21
museum, 2-22
music
must
mutual, 5-17
my
myself
mystery, 1-22
myth, 6-21

nail, 4-7
naked, 3-4
name
narrative, 6-2
narrow, 2-10
nation, 3-20
native, 4-4
natural, 2-14
navy, 1-18
near
nearby, 2-3
nearby, 4-14
neat, 4-1
necessary
necessary, 3-1
neck, 3-19
need
needle, 4-10
negative, 3-7
neglect, 5-17
negotiate, 3-2
neighbor
neighborhood, 1-3
neither, 3-7
nephew, 2-5
nest, 4-19
net, 6-8

never
nevertheless, 6-23
new
news
newspaper
next
nice
niece, 2-5
night
nightmare, 3-12
nine
no
no one
nobody
nod, 4-24
noise
noise, 2-1
none
nonflammable, 5-21
nonsense, 5-24
noon, 1-8
normal, 3-19
north
nose
not
note, 2-1
nothing
notice, 4-8
notion, 6-8
nourishment, 6-3
novel, 3-1, 6-10
now
nowadays, 2-20
nowhere
nucleus, 5-12
nude, 5-15
number
numerous, 3-12
nurse, 1-14, 5-7
nursery, 6-2
nursery school, 6-2
nut, 4-16
nutritious, 5-11

obey, 4-17
object, 2-21
object, 3-6, 6-4
objective, 6-10
obligation, 5-17
observe, 5-25
obstacle, 4-21
obtain, 4-14
obvious, 2-20

occasion, 3-25
occupation, 3-2
occupy, 4-4, 6-20
occur, 2-10, 4-17
ocean
o'clock
odd, 1-25, 6-14
odds, 5-20
odor, 6-3
of
of course, 2-21
off
offend, 5-17
offer, 3-2
office
officer, 2-8, 6-12
officer, 6-16
official, 2-11
offspring, 6-15
often
oil, 2-16, 5-11
old
omit, 5-4
on
once
one
only
open
operation, 4-17
operator, 1-24
opinion, 1-20
opportunity, 5-13
opposition, 3-18
oppress, 6-4
optics, 6-24
optimistic, 4-3
optimum, 5-3
optional, 4-1
or
orally, 5-2
orange, 3-11
orchestra, 1-9
order, 2-11, 2-21, 5-15
ordinary, 3-25
ore, 6-9
organ, 6-17
organic, 6-24
organize, 4-19
oriental, 3-22
orientation, 4-1
original, 2-21
orphan, 4-18
other
otherwise, 3-25

sky, **1**-4
slave, **6**-15
sleep
slide, **3**-12
slight, **3**-25
slip, **4**-8
slope, **6**-8
slow
slow down, **6**-22
slow up, **6**-22
small
smart, **3**-23
smell, **3**-15
smile
smoke, **2**-16
smooth, **3**-12
snack, **5**-11
snake, **2**-18
sneak **5**-22
snow
so
soap
soccer, **2**-14
socialism, **5**-1
society, **4**-12
sock, **2**-9
soft, **4**-8
soil, **4**-11
solar, **4**-9
soldier, **1**-18
solid, **2**-15
solution, **3**-6
some
somebody
somehow
someone
something
sometimes
somewhere
son
song
soon
sophisticated, **6**-7
sore, **5**-8, **5**-23
sorry
sort, **5**-5
sound, **2**-23
soup
source, **3**-17
south
space, **1**-12, **6**-24
spare, **6**-13
spark, **5**-21
sparse, **6**-15

speak
special, **2**-12
species, **5**-16
specify, **4**-14
specimen, **6**-24
speech, **1**-20
speed, **3**-3
spell
spell out, **6**-10
spend
sphere, **6**-24
spill, **4**-19
spirit, **4**-20
spiritual, **4**-20
split, **6**-22
sponsor, **6**-2
spoon
sport
spot, **3**-4, **5**-21
spread, **6**-3
spring
spring up, **5**-13
stable, **4**-12
staff, **3**-2
stage, **5**-18
stain, **5**-15
stairs, **2**-25
stamp, **1**-6
stand
stand by, **5**-21
stand for, **6**-10
stand out, **6**-16
stand up, **6**-5, **6**-19
stand up for, **6**-1
stand up to, **6**-1
standard, **4**-14
standpoint, **6**-10
star, **4**-19
stare, **2**-23
start
starve, **5**-11
state, **3**-2, **5**-1
station, **1**-2, **6**-22
statistics, **5**-12
status, **6**-20
stay, **1**-7
steady, **4**-8
steal, **1**-22
stealthy, **5**-21
steel, **4**-2
steep, **4**-24
step, **3**-16
step aside, **5**-1
sterile, **6**-17

stick, **3**-5
stick, **4**-19
stick to, **6**-8
stick up for, **6**-9
still, **6**-22
stimulate, **6**-24
stir, **4**-16
stock, **4**-14
stocking, **5**-15
stomach, **1**-16
stone
stop
store/storage, **1**-12
storm, **1**-4
story
stove, **2**-4
straight, **4**-2
strain, **6**-22
strange, **1**-23
strategy, **6**-20
street
strength, **2**-14
stress, **3**-2
stretch, **4**-10
strict, **3**-22
strike, **3**-24, **5**-19
string, **4**-11
strip, **6**-11
strong
structure, **5**-6
struggle, **5**-9
student
study
stuff, **6**-11
stuffy, **6**-11
stupid, **4**-17
style, **4**-10
subject
subject, **2**-17
submerge, **6**-9
submissive, **5**-5, **6**-21
submit, **5**-5, **6**-21
subordinate, **6**-16
subsequent, **5**-8
substance, **3**-6
substantial, **6**-25
substitute, **4**-1
subtract, **3**-13
suburb, **1**-12
succeed, **1**-10
such
suffer, **4**-8
sufficient, **2**-16
sugar

Index

Words in Volume 7

Numbers refers to **volume** and unit. The letter "p" or "r" after an entry indicates whether the word is in the *Words for Production* (p) or *Words for Recognition* (r) section of the unit.